EARLY ACCLAIM FOR
THE POWER OF PEACE IN YOU

My greatest influences regarding prayer and meditation are Dr. Wayne Dyer, Deepak Chopra, Eckhart Tolle, Lama Surya Das, and Marlise Karlin. I feel moved to mention that a course with Marlise, in particular, generated amazing results in my life. Her instruction enabled me to open my heart up as never before. ~ **Robert Radcliffe**, Author of *180 Degrees*

* * *

The Power of Peace in You is unlike any book I have read; it offers easy, accessible techniques that I use daily. Marlise writes in an authentic, touching, and poetic manner that leads the reader on a compelling journey, initiated when this energy entered her body and began eliminating anything that separated her from her potential as an awakened conscious human being. *The Power of Peace in You* remarkably and simply demonstrates how this potential is available to all of us. ~ **James Egan**, Award-Winning Producer, *Angels in the Dust*, *Kimjongilia*

* * *

Through Marlise we recognize that this gift of consciousness is not so distant after all… and as we embrace this new potential, we are able to move towards a new global dialogue that just may contribute something very special indeed to the future of life on Earth. ~ **Wade Davis**, Ph.D Ethnobotany, Harvard, Author of 17 books including *One River*

* * *

For most of us our conscious mind has only a very small information channel capacity and thus we are mostly asleep. However, for those topics for which it gives meaning, our unconscious mind, with over a million times that information channel capacity, feeds it digestible kernels of information to help inspire the conscious mind's growth and action in those particular areas. The teachings of Marlise Karlin's body of work give meaning to the most important sources of wisdom available to our world. ~ **William A. Tiller**, Ph.D, featured scientist on *What The Bleep Do We Know*

* * *

The old saying, "The person is the message" is so true today. Marlise is her message. She has lived it, done it, and dealt with some of life's most difficult challenges as she has developed and validated it. Her purpose is to help others as she has been helped. Her passion is limitless. Her power flows from the deepest of sincere hearts. ~ **Ron Willingham**, Chairman and Founder of LifeScript Learning

* * *

Marlise is one of the brightest lights in the world today, transforming the lives of everyone she encounters. The energy she transmits ignites and awakens the power of peace within your heart and inspires you to live the conscious power-full life you deserve. Marlise shows you how to heal yourself from the inside out, simply and effectively. She is a shining gift to us all. ~ **Cari Murphy**, Coach and Media Host

* * *

Thank you for taking your time to introduce your method among our team. I would like to incorporate Stillness into the training curriculum of doctors, and nurses, and counselors who work in the HIV/AIDS services in Cambodia. ~ **Dr. SOK Thim**, Executive Director of Cambodian Health Committee

* * *

Marlise is a fearless conduit for Divine love who has dedicated her life to providing individuals access to the greatest treasure of all... themselves. ~ **Panache Desai**, Inspirational Visionary

* * *

Marlise Karlin experienced a sudden life-altering awakening that connected her to what she refers to as the Energy of peace. This unassuming woman with an exuberant laugh believes this happened so she could share it with others. This journey of discovery is here for anyone who seeks to know it for themselves in *The Power of Peace in You*. There is so much beauty and soul in Marlise's words they vibrate with Stillness. What a wonderful impossibility! ~ **Martin Hughes**, Former Managing Director of *Yogi Times*

* * *

Marlise's stories instilled in me a tsunami of love, peace, and truth... so immediate, so intense—it was like a force of nature. Most books do not transmit this transcendent Stillness and abundance of Energy. I was connected. ~ **David Stone**, U.K.

* * *

I have had many teachers attempt to move me to that place—but Marlise and her work made it *now!* How great is it that during the day when your mind is chattering about a thousand things—you can remember her technique and access the Power in you at any moment. And the result is—that the world changes! This is a new work for a new time. ~ **Pavel Mikoloski**, U.S.A.

* * *

After reading only the first three chapters of *The Power of Peace in You*, I have made a profound shift in myself already. Anyone, who is sincere about discovering and uncovering their true nature, can only benefit from engaging with the words and practices in this book. What an opportunity for growth! This book is profound and powerful. ~ **Tarlach O'Maolain**, Ireland

* * *

After reading only a portion of the book, and listening to the Stillness Session, I had some amazing breakthroughs. I literally saw some old parts of myself/patterns dissolving. I am grateful to be finding my SELF, my strength, my voice...with confidence and grace. It was a beautiful and powerful experience. ~ **Kristen Hundley**, U.S.A.

* * *

Thank you so much for this gift you have shown me. I cannot even compare the person I was to the person I am now. The Simplicity of Stillness has given me the opportunity to rearrange my priorities without fear that I will be "losing something". I can't wait to see where Stillness takes me the rest of my life and how I can teach my future children about it! ~ **Shauna Burke**, Chef, Colorado, U.S.

to anyone who has ever had a moment
of not feeling loved
or didn't feel worthy of being loved.

to anyone who was ever told that you couldn't have
the dream that was written on your heart,
that you couldn't let go of the addiction
that had a hold of you,
or that you couldn't become the person
you knew you were...

this book is for you

you are loved beyond what you can imagine...
once you experience this Love,
you'll be free to live your dreams,
and be all that you know
you truly are.

THE POWER OF
PEACE IN YOU

Distributed in the USA and Canada by Sterling Publishing Co., Inc.
387 Park Avenue South, New York, NY 10016-8810

This edition first published in the USA 2012 by
Watkins Publishing, Sixth Floor, Castle House,
75–76 Wells Street, London W1T 3QH

10 9 8 7 6 5 4 3 2 1

Edited by Joanna Pyle
Copy-edited by Merryl Lentz and Shelagh Boyd
Design by YoungJu Lee

Manufactured in the United States of America

Library of Congress Cataloging-in-Publication Data Available

ISBN: 978-1-78028-382-1

For information about custom editions, special sales, premium and corporate purchases,
please contact Sterling Special Sales Department at 800-805-5489 or specialsales@
sterlingpub.com

The Simplicity of Stillness® and Stillness Sessions® are registered trademarks
of Inner Knowing International Inc.
Inner Knowing International Inc., 1539 W Sawtelle Blvd Ste 4, Los Angeles,
California 90025
www.marlisekarlin.com

www.watkinspublishing.co.uk

THE POWER OF PEACE IN YOU

A revolutionary tool for
Hope, Healing and Happiness
in the 21st Century

marlise karlin

WATKINS PUBLISHING
LONDON

TABLE OF CONTENTS

PART 4
THE JOURNEY
HEALING
INTEGRATION
EMPOWERMENT

PART 5
WHERE DO WE GO FROM HERE?
CONSCIOUS LIVING

FOREWORD

If there is one truth that I have been able to distill from my travels it is the realization that every culture at some profound level seeks a closer connection and a deeper understanding of the divine. The urge to elevate the spirit, to invoke some technique of ecstasy that will momentarily place the individual in an altered state of consciousness is so ubiquitous in the anthropological record that it must surely be seen as a fundamental human desire.

Bearing witness to transformative ritual has always left me in awe; from a Buddhist monk pursuing the breath of the dharma, to Jaguar shamans in the Amazon ingesting ayahuasca. I never imagined that one day I would gain a deeper understanding of this state of consciousness while sitting on a bus in Polynesia.

I had hoped to steal a few moments of quiet, but my mind was consumed by a dozen irritations, nothing particularly serious, just the general clutter many of us allow to scatter our attentions and cloud our hearts. Suddenly two hands gently placed headphones on my ears. Marlise appeared behind me, with a smile that seemed say, 'Maybe this will help...'

I had no idea what was about to transpire. It was my first exposure to what I now think of as Marlise's gift to the world, a unique and disarming method of inner work and liberation that has transformed people's lives globally for the last ten years.

The music and words in the recording were harmonious and balanced, transcendent and yet grounded in some impulse that drew me like a lodestone. Time was suspended, when I opened my eyes, I could suddenly see the idyllic setting that was right in front of me, yet completely hidden from view because of my previous state of mind.

In the days to follow, I found myself going into stillness, listening to her recording over and over, and every day seemed to unfold another level of depth and intuition. *Stillness Sessions* became a constant companion wherever I traveled. I never grew tired of them, nor did I exhaust the potential of Marlise's message, which impressed me as being all the more powerful and profound precisely because of its apparent yet deceptive simplicity.

At times I found myself being introspective, I became aware of what stopped me from being more open and empathetic – maybe I didn't listen to people as deeply and patiently as I could. Suddenly I was able to clear up a deep rift with a lost friend. At other moments I was joyous and effervescent. It was like being able to breathe again, and there was a lightness to my spirit that I hadn't known for a long time. Each new awareness offered me a lens through which to see the world where problems became adventures to be dealt with in new ways.

I wasn't the only person affected by Marlise's presence and the fathomless energy stream that emanates through her and illumines her work. With the same grace she brought to teaching inner-city kids in America, Maasai warriors in the Serengeti, and traditional healers in Bali, she opened the hearts of men and women on our journey who had achieved the kind of success that in our culture generally leads, if anything, to a closing of the mind and soul. What she shared through the teachings of her methodology and what she calls 'the energy of peace' allowed them to embrace their humanity, resulting in a shift among the group as a whole, where they instinctively became more caring and respectful of one another.

People respond in part because Marlise so clearly comes from a place of authenticity. As she reveals in this book, her life has not always been easy: I believe this is what makes her words and work so accessible. Through her we recognize that this gift of consciousness is not so distant after all. We begin to let go of ideas and behaviors that create separation, and as we embrace this new potential, we are able to move towards a new global dialogue that just may contribute something very special indeed to the future of life on Earth.

As we shed old attachments and patterns of behavior, Marlise urges us not to abandon this world as much as to allow ourselves to be called into another. Touched by the stunning clarity of luminous love, she articulates a path of transformation even as she offers a methodology that people from all cultures can embrace in a process of transformation and illumination.

Marlise's words carry a spark that resonates deeply in the heart of all of us, and her stories of people who embraced these truths will, I believe, inspire you as they did me. When His Holiness the Thirteenth Dalai Lama was once asked to name his spiritual peers, he responded, "Everyone!" We are all instruments in the heart of humanity. It's time for more people to live in a deeper understanding of our essential nature. *The Power of Peace in You* offers the roadmap; now all that's left to do, is get on the bus.

Wade Davis, Author of 14 books including *One River*,
Nat Geo Explorer, PhD Ethnobotany; Harvard University

PREFACE

On a misty morning in November of 2001 I awoke with a paralyzing sadness that seemed to penetrate every part of me. The thoughts crowding my mind sent spirals of incomprehensible shame and anxiety into my brain. *How could I have done so many horrible things in my life? I'll never know the love and peace I want… I'm not worthy… I'm not… I'm not even worthy of forgiveness…* Everything I had dreamed of for so long – now seemed impossible. The hopelessness I felt was overwhelming.

Tears flowed into uncaring pillows that couldn't comfort me. Nothing seemed to matter. Not even the beauty surrounding me: the art on the walls or the glistening ocean that shimmered across the sandy beach in front of my home. Even the usual calming resonance of waves lapping on the shore was drowned out by my sorrowful cries. It was all so meaningless. *How did I get here? Why was this happening?*

My life had been one of many colors from youth. At 16 I painted my bedroom walls black from the pain I felt growing up with an abusive alcoholic parent. But the feelings surfacing now weren't about my childhood. What tormented me now were years of my transgressions. I watched as the screen of my mind vividly displayed the unconscious choices I had made. Doing cocaine night after night. Dancing for a living in bars. Using sex like a drug because it made me feel like I was finally in control. Drinking, drinking, and more drinking. Rainbowed hues of desolation streamed one visual after the next through my broken heart. And the tears continued to rain down.

The promise of the unimagined, the freedom and contentment that streams from knowing absolute peace – was becoming an elusive dream again... though I believed with all my heart it was possible. My years of study with a lineage of meditation masters, Baba Muktananda[1] and Gurumayi Chidvilasananda[2], becoming the International Director of their Foundation and traveling the world, plus years assimilating the teachings of Mary Burmeister[3], a master of Jin Shin Jyutsu, a renowned ancient healing tradition, and absorbing the knowledge of the many evolutionary teachers who followed in fields as diverse as quantum science, principled leadership, alternative healing disciplines, and the laws of attraction – had inspired within me a recognition that *what I believed was possible – was*. We could access the life force Energy that would grant us a greater understanding of our innate potential – not in another lifetime; we could know it now – and by synthesizing all I had studied, I *believed* the processes would connect me with this experience. And yet, here I was, seemingly at a lower rung of the ladder than I'd been for years.

Even the achievement and success that followed my early struggles were no consolation. National Director of a non-profit organization, CEO and award-winning film producer, interior architectural designer of extraordinary homes, having a loving husband – all empty images appearing on a mantle of small significance in comparison to where I had turned my search – to live in connection with that eloquent power of peace. My enthusiasm had become a gnawing empty ache. I felt so alone...

you don't even know… what you don't know… until…
Suddenly, a palpable stream of *Energy* began to move through me; it was unlike anything I had known, including my initial *awakening* experience with Baba. Words can't begin to describe the sensations of luminous love resonating throughout my body. As deeper levels of pain from my past began dissolving, light streamed into my vision literally and figuratively. Sadness turned to wonder and awe. And even though I had been on a 20-year journey into knowing deep truths, *this was so much more than anything I had ever thought possible. My perception of life was forever changed.*

As my understanding evolved, my life transformed as well. Access to this field of awareness began to soften challenges of daily uncertainty. Strengths appeared that inspired new decisions – fear and anxiety dissipated. I wondered if this would be a onetime occurrence to reflect on in my later years. Answers soon arrived; the experiences multiplied, and my mind and body continued to heal, becoming highly energized and revitalized.

This stream of pure peace had ignited an expanded connection into higher consciousness where the Love that exists for all of us offered me clarity of purpose. My capacity for love seemed to overflow daily beyond the intermittent play of only now and then. The teachings were experiential rather than conceptual. The mind is a powerful assistant, but it can't offer what is available once this timeless dimension elaborates the knowledge of the heart; this is the place where you ask the logical mind to be quiet because your creative heart/mind has begun expanding your world in ways you never dreamed possible. The benefits proved to not only be for *my* benefit but for everyone who came into this energy field now resonating powerfully through me.

the energy sea of unquantifiable peace

What we usually reference as *energy* is not what this is. This expansion of consciousness in form offers access to a higher intelligence that can be integrated into the everyday of life – and, there is nothing you have to believe in, it's *experiential* – and, as more research today reveals, cognizance without experience is not all that helpful. I felt the alchemy this Energy initiated as a constant *hummm* coursing through my body. The many talents we have that are not known to us without gaining access to this field of potential were revealed through events created to demonstrate my new capabilities. Many scientists have researched this *quantum sea of Energy*, which Lynn McTaggart writes about in her remarkably informative book, *The Field*.[4]

Dr Jill Bolte Taylor, a Harvard-trained neuroanatomist, gained insight beyond the normal limits of human perception while having a stroke. She observed herself being in a state of *inner peace* that she had not recognized existed. In her book, *My Stroke of Insight,* Jill reported this experience to be of a physical nature that pierced the paralyzed state she was in.[5] This extremely perilous event gave her access to an experience beyond the constraints of everyday reality as most people know it. What an amazing gift to receive! How very sad it would be if having a stroke was our only recourse to this profound connection. It isn't.

In the years following that cataclysmic window into the very nature of our essence, I discovered how to access this pulse of life immediately and consistently, so the benefits would be available, not just when feeling depleted, but for adding fuel to the overall purpose of my life. I spent my days reflecting and integrating the awareness that continued opening in greater depth – releasing layers of limiting beliefs, learning to forgive, trust, and live in the joy of creation. And any time I got stuck I discovered answers by using the methods I had developed from years of research and application, editing out what wasn't simplistic while incorporating the treasures culled from each field of education studied.

I dedicated myself to developing a comprehensive methodology that would bring the two worlds together, *this profound* Energy and *the practical* processes that integrated this form of higher learning into life. I wanted it to be so simple that anyone could benefit; people who had been on a longtime journey as I had, as well as those who were just starting out. I believe the statement, *The future belongs to a very different kind of person with a very different kind of mind...* is true. Maybe this could be a way for the logical part of us to be fused with the creative heart/mind knowing I was experiencing. In the years to come I became an active participant in all that I was meant to understand – and The Simplicity of Stillness Method was born.

new voyages of discovery
What I witnessed as I traveled the globe sealed my commitment to sharing this new paradigm for higher learning. I wanted to fully comprehend how it was possible for something that appeared this simple, to bridge so many different lifestyles, and effect such rapid transformation in a person's life. People who had experienced the trauma we are all witness to, as well as those who had endured the unspeakable – connected to their innate power using this methodology and it completely shifted the trajectory of their lives.

From Maasai warriors in Kenya to CEOs in Amsterdam, from children in Papua, New Guinea to doctors in Europe – all cultures and ages found the hope they needed to face life's many setbacks and the inspiration to empower a future filled with possibility. Kids dealing with the heartache and anguish of being bullied discovered their self-worth, teens healed their eating disorders, and adults found self-love after years of chronic depression. The stories in this book are about some of these extraordinary people who walked through a maze of challenges and found the wisdom, courage, and confidence to share their talents with others through their unique expression.

We are all instruments in the heart of humankind, and can learn to embrace our frailties as well as our greatness – which is how I learned to accept that I would become a teacher of this extraordinary gift when I had lived such an *imperfect* life myself. When I recognized it was possible for anyone to leave their past suffering behind, find hope and live from the experience of their innate potential and greatness – it touched me deeply, and became the genesis of the humanitarian work I do today.

The Simplicity of Stillness Method ignites and expands an infinite power within you to recognize your greatest potential. It is not the *only* way; anyone who ever tells you that… run… fast! It's time for old concepts like these to perish. We are all instruments for bringing the light of consciousness into the world, and we can each choose to allow this dimension of life to be conveyed through us – or not. As you take this voyage of discovery into the very nature of what is possible in the 21st century, I can promise you that this timeless intelligence will guide you, day by day, choice by choice, experience by experience into a reality that is filled with the joy of living and a clarity of purpose.

It isn't a theory, it is the evolution of humankind that I

have been witness to, and this book is the emergence of the guidance received. The promise it offers makes what appears complex, simple. Reclaiming your innate power and expanding peace throughout the world – inner and outer – is possible, and it's more accessible now than ever before. It's the journey of a lifetime, and I am so happy to be taking it with you.

With Great Love,

Marlise

INTRODUCTION

Imagine a situation where you are surrounded by chaos: people are rushing around, everyone is talking at the same time, fueled by their own anxiety or purpose, and moving at lightning speed. You are in the midst of it all, and not influenced by it. In spite of the pandemonium, you are in a place of complete clarity and equanimity – magnified by your experience of the power of peace in you. This is not a conceptual mindset, but a depth of knowing that you recognize as it expands within. This is a *knowing* that enlightens your daily decisions, and inspires a way of being that is resilient, intuitive, creative, courageous, and caring.

We have arrived at a time in our history when change is imminent, where many people are feeling that stirring from within, inviting them to be part of a greater conversation evolving into a society of more highly conscious individuals. The Simplicity of Stillness Method is a roadmap into this world, a new way of being, where we live connected to what we value most. It's a reality that is possible now, not in some distant future when we have more time, or we've handled our crises of the moment, or our karma is better. That future is here now.

In 2004 I began traveling the world, igniting this Energy of peace in people of every culture. I personally witnessed how the power that resonates through us when we are connected to higher intelligence – transforms lives – our own, as well as the lives of others. As this alchemy of truth ignites or expands within, we can participate in healing our unconscious behaviors and significantly impact the course of our life, as well as the precarious global challenges we all face today.

The Simplicity of Stillness incorporates *the profound* into *the practical*; it is an advanced methodology to match the time we are in and the new era we are moving into. It is not aligned with any religion or spiritual path, and is inclusive of all. Included here are some basic principles that will be helpful to understand as the *invisible* Energy of consciousness in this methodology, becomes more verifiable. Let's start with *the profound*.

the profound

What I discovered through the integration of the profound energetic experiences that transformed my life is somewhat paradoxical. While this Energy of higher intelligence is beyond the senses, we can attune to it through sound, sight, touch, and intention (more about this in 'Laying the Foundation'). Contradictory as this may sound, there is scientific evidence today that demonstrates this understanding. Researchers have established that there is Energy connecting every living entity. In other words, the apparent separation between us is more accurately evidence of something unseen. That *something unseen* is a conscious Energy. Electromagnetic fields broadcast and communicate within the body at a cellular level, as well as outside our body. Every living thing registers these signals.

Ervin Laszlo, the brilliant author of 74 books translated into 20 languages, nominated twice for the Nobel Peace Prize, describes this mysterious Energy sea as the quantum vacuum, 'This field is not outside of nature: it is the heart of nature.

It is the originating ground of all things in the universe, and also their ultimate destination.'[1] He further explains how 'In ages past, the connectedness and wholeness of the world was known to medicine men, priests, shamans, seers and sages, and to all people who had the courage to look beyond their nose and stay open to what they saw... Now in the first decade of the 21st century, innovative scientists at the frontiers of science are rediscovering the integral nature of reality.'[2]

Whether you simply want peace of mind and balance in your life, or to connect with the light-filled realms written about in ancient texts[3], this Energy ignites an expansion of the innate potential that exists within every human being.

the practical

Integrating The Simplicity of Stillness Method into the everyday of life is where the rubber meets the road. This is not an esoteric conversation that dissipates into ethers the moment a baby cries, you lose your job, or an important relationship in your life changes. If you can't take the highest teachings into your life, what good would they be? You'll find qualities that are synonymous with this higher vibration impacting your every thought and action: enthusiasm, inspiration, forgiveness, kindness, cheerfulness, and a general sense of well-being.

The *practical* involves walking this journey with the intention of connecting to your very soul *and* dealing with your greatest challenges, inviting whatever has been hidden – to be revealed. Will your world suddenly be free of all troubles? Of course not, but you will know how to process them through a lens of greater clarity that brings better outcomes. Concepts once seen as *truth* become free of obscurity, *stories* once thought to be *the way it is* are revealed as illusion. Every day you'll notice difficulties you might once have considered daunting now being handled with a sense of ease.

influencing the future from the now

Our thoughts and actions matter; they are essential in creating our lives, and the world we wish to live in. Every intention is heard in the field of universal intelligence. As the energy of focused thought is sent into a quantum field, it has the organizing power to bring fulfillment.

In his book, *There's a Spiritual Solution to Every Problem*, beloved teacher and bestselling author Wayne Dyer, wrote about this vibrational energy field that contains the solutions to our problems. 'They [scientists] study matter at the subatomic level and report that the essence of creation is energy.'[4] Dyer continues this conversation, 'As you begin to consider this idea of faster vibrations being synonymous with spirit, remind yourself that we live in a world of invisible energy that we take for granted. Electromagnetic forces all operate on vibrational frequencies that we cannot see, smell or touch.'[5]

Dr Valerie V Hunt affirms this theory in her book, *Infinite Mind*, reporting that when a person's field reached higher vibrational states, 'He experienced knowing higher information, transcendental ideas, insight about ultimate sources of reality, and creativity in its purest form. Thoughts were grander, more penetrating and global.'[6]

igniting the power of peace in you

This book's promise is to offer you a way to connect with this Energy stream of pure peace through a simple and profound method that aligns with your personal truth. The Power of Peace Map is a visual guide with signposts that appear as you walk your way through the book.

Part 1 invites you to set an intention so you are dynamically involved and fully participating in the heart/mind vision you have claimed.

Part 2 is immediately experiential. Simply by listening to the Stillness Session accompanying this book, charged with that energetic stream of consciousness, life begins to transform – and all you are doing, in effect, is listening to beautiful music.

Part 3 lays the foundation for understanding the basic tenets and how remarkably these diverse schools of thought coalesce: modern scientific studies with ancient scriptural teachings, healing disciplines, and my own experiences and observations of what is possible when this Energy sea of intelligence is accessed.

Part 4 details the journey, laying out a context within each chapter that defines each step, and includes stories of people who accessed this powerful universal force and created their lives anew. And, each chapter ends with a Simplicity of Stillness (SOS) Practice that you can immediately incorporate into your own life.

Part 5 sets the stage for what is possible as each one of us incorporates the conscious wisdom available today and shares it with our world community.

If we can use the galvanizing force of this infinite intelligence to intend, realize, and illumine what humans have searched for throughout time, just imagine what is possible. Wade Davis, gifted anthropologist, ethnobotanist, and visionary, says it beautifully in *The Wayfinders*, 'Each one of us is a chapter in the greatest story ever written, a narrative of exploration and discovery remembered not only in myth but encoded in our blood. Every cell in our bodies is charged by a miracle… that

helps orchestrate every pulse of sentient existence.'[7]
We are all that pulse, that living miracle. As you incorporate The Simplicity of Stillness Method into your life, the inherent power of that Energy will invite you – to rediscover this exquisite knowing within yourself... moment-by-moment, day-by-day, experience-by-experience.

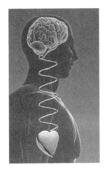

Intention

Setting your
Heart/Mind
Vision

Experience

Igniting the Power
of Infinite Peace

Knowledge

Calming &
Expanding
the Mind

Healing

Healing Blockages,
Establishing New
Beliefs

POWER OF PEACE MAP

Integration

Acquiring Empowered
Habits, Behaviors &
Actions

Empowerment

Consistent Inspired
Choices Reflect
Quality of Life

Conscious Living

Fulfillment, Freedom
& Peace

THE CONVERGENCE OF KNOWLEDGE & EXPERIENCE
A New Paradigm for Learning in the 21st Century

How do you explain the most *profound* mysteries of our time and develop them into a simple method that is accessible to people of every age and culture? The answer is: *Through the convergence of intellectual knowledge with experiential wisdom.* Within the pages of *The Power of Peace in You* is a roadmap that demonstrates how we can bring these two seemingly disparate worlds together. The fundamental way we have viewed learning is being redefined today by the accelerated possibilities that technology is presenting us – *and* through a growing movement employing the intelligence of the creative heart/mind to initiate an advanced cooperative society that is driven by value, meaning, and purpose.

How *the profound*, an indefinably powerful and innate gift of peace, can be integrated into *the practical* of everyday will change how we see and do just about everything. Over 25 years of research, study, and application, synthesizing ancient meditation traditions, healing disciplines, and evolutionary schools of thought, with the alchemical nature of the life force Energy I was experiencing, resulted in the development of The Simplicity of Stillness (SOS) methodology.

This experiential form of education could become one of the most innovative for evolutionary learning in the 21st century because people access an accelerated awareness that radically shifts limiting behavior patterns – and invites the *retention* of what they aspire to understand. Our life circumstances won't change significantly solely through intellectual knowledge. For this to occur, we have to change our behavior, which results when our inner beliefs are transformed. And, since retention is widely recognized as a perennial weak spot for most new learning, both of these elements necessitate a pivotal part of the transformative trajectory of personal fulfillment and empowerment.

According to Ron Willingham[1], 'We live in an intellectual world where we view education as dispensing information. Nevertheless, 21 days after we hear information, we promptly forget up to 95% of it.' Ron is the Founder of Integrity Systems and has spent the majority of his life helping people and organizations lead value-driven lives, training more than 1.5 million graduates in 80 nations. His years of expertise have shown him:

when our inner beliefs change, so does our behavior

Behavioral change is a dynamic experiential process. My life's study has provided me with extraordinary evidence of how accelerated learning occurs when people include an *experiential* connection to the Energy of infinite intelligence. Tapping into this power shifts your very perception of life, which, of course, includes the inner beliefs we have that block our ability to live at our highest potential. Over the last years, countless people who experienced the difference this form of education brought them, emphatically questioned: *Why aren't we taught this in school?? This is the most important education you can get. It changes everything.*

Daniel H Pink, *New York Times* bestselling author of *A Whole New Mind: Why Right Brainers Will Rule the Future*[2] says, 'The future belongs to a very different kind of person with a very different kind of mind'. His research suggests that left-brain dominance might have reached the end of its reign, and that incorporating right-brain creative thinking is the wave of the future. The question to consider is: how can we bring these worlds together and fully integrate a heart/mind, logical/ creative way of learning, living, and being?

In *The Power of Peace in You* the educational process begins with setting a heart/mind vision of what you *really* value and want out of life, then having an *experience* of the deep truths that can bring this intention into reality. The next step invites you to dive into the *knowledge* of how this is possible – calming and expanding the mind from being in conflict with its natural egocentric thinking, taking you to the integrative practices where behavioral changes occur and natural empowerment arises, evidenced by the thousands of extraordinary people who have walked this journey. You'll find some of their stories in the pages of this book: from business professionals in Europe, to tribal communities in Africa, from inner-city kids in the USA, to doctors in hospitals in Asia.

By including the core elements of this cohesive methodology in your life, Stillness Sessions, The Three Breath Awareness and The SOS Practices, the results needn't be short-lived. *The Power of Peace in You* offers you tools to develop empowered, lasting change. Conscious living is the result – and the next steps you take to assure its translation into the world at large is what *you* will define through the retention and access you discover – through the *inherent knowing* in you.

we are not here to move to the mountaintops.
we are here to live our lives, to work and dream and play
to be with our children, to be with one another and
to come together as a world community.

we are here to live in the knowing of the peace
once found only in those lofty silent spaces... and
to bring it now into each moment of our daily lives.

1

SETTING YOUR HEART/MIND VISION

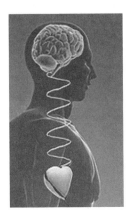

INTENTION

What's at stake is your life. If you aren't aiming at what you want your life to be about, you are just managing the busyness of it all... year after year. Why not have an overview, and be willing to adjust as your life's purpose comes into play. You will set many Intentions in your life... there is no *perfect* one, there is only the one that you are setting *now*... and it is absolutely perfect.

Creating your Intention from a place of connection between your heart and mind will generate inspired enthusiasm, passion for life, and an increased enjoyment of the abundance arriving in every form: beauty, prosperity, loving relationships, work that is meaningful, and the recognition that you make a difference – just by being you.

SETTING YOUR HEART/MIND VISION

Begin with the end in mind,[1] Contemplate your death to know how to live your life[2], and *Leave your ego with your shoes at the door[3]* are all brilliant ways of making a similar point – there is a new way of getting where you want to go – and these insights are signposts leading the way.

Begin now by setting a heart/mind vision or an intention of what you *really* want out of life, keeping the thoughts above as inspiration of what you hope to find: a loving quality, peace of mind, release from blockages that cause suffering, or even what you want your life to have been about when you are reviewing it from a rocking chair in your later years:

_____

_____

_____

_____

_____

Now you have reached that perfect time to dive into the experiential part of this journey that can assist you in bringing your vision into reality... and all you have to do... is just turn the page.

2

IGNITING THE POWER OF PEACE

EXPERIENCE

This book's process is dynamic and is intended to be experiential. Intellectual knowledge rarely impacts your inner beliefs or unconscious behavior in a way that causes you to take action and develop new habits that are enduring.

The dimension of life you want to expand opens through the gateway of personal experience. As you connect with universal intelligence through the Energy of infinite peace it affects your unconscious beliefs, releases limiting patterns, and opens pathways for higher learning – generating new life circumstances that are in harmony with your highest aspirations.

IGNITING THE ENERGY
OF INFINITE PEACE

It's always the perfect time to experience healing Stillness and the infinite Energy of peace. Listening to a Stillness Session where the words and music resonate that loving intelligence, you ignite a deeper knowing of your greatest potential and the depth of peace within your heart.

To enhance your experience listen on headphones. Find a quiet space where you can lie down – or just sit in a comfortable position where you are in this moment. Holding on to that heart/mind vision of what you are *really* wanting… let everything slow down… let the world drift away… then…

Lower the Lights…

Switch off the World…

Listen…

The Power of Peace Stillness Session CD can be found at the back of the book.

When you change the prescription of your glasses the world becomes clearer. Invite the knowledge within the pages of this book to bring you an even greater expression of your innate gifts and the peace you have always wanted to know. 'Laying the Foundation' can entrain that expansion and calming of the mind. And, if you have sincerely *left your shoes at the door,* you are ready to begin.

3
LAYING THE
FOUNDATION

KNOWLEDGE
Calming & Expanding the Mind

Feeding the mind so it will support your choices in life and not fight or resist them is extremely important. When the tape recording in your head is stuck on *you're not good enough*, or what you want *is impossible* – finding evidence to support the new beliefs that are resonating from your conscious awareness is key.

This chapter offers you a new paradigm for all future educational endeavors. Innovative solutions are needed to develop lasting peace in every area of life. They can be found through the synchronization of *experience* – with *knowledge* – with *inspired action*.

You are the master of your destiny, who you BE determines your life experience, and application of an experiential process, like The Simplicity of Stillness Method, could be the determining factor that brings you your heart's desire.

LEARNING, LIVING, LOVING: THE EVOLUTION OF THE SIMPLICITY OF STILLNESS METHOD

Will it give me peace of mind? Can it support me in my daily life, help me study, and become more focused? Can it give me the courage I need to face life's challenges? And, can it just help me sleep? Yes, yes, yes… and so much more. From scientific journals to Time Magazine and an array of published books, scientists and doctors around the world have published an abundance of data on the remarkable physiological and psychological benefits of meditation. When individuals I worked with began observing and hearing from people around the world who had incorporated The Simplicity of Stillness Method into their lives, we were amazed at the dramatic benefits evidenced that characterized similar, and yet often an accelerated effectiveness.

There is only one field of conscious awareness; is it possible a process could expedite the benefits – by transmitting this life force Energy in a way that could be integrated more simply than ever before? And is it also an indication that demonstrates how this dimension of consciousness is more accessible at this time in history than ever before? I believe both are among the unifying elements arising now to create an awakening of immense proportions.

how the emergence of SOS came to be…

To reconstruct how The Simplicity of Stillness methodology was born, let me take you back in time. In 2004, after realizing I was meant to impart this alchemy of pure Energy, questions appeared that elicited the uncommon answers I began receiving. This *conscious* Energy stream, *the profound* element of The SOS Method, would be transmitted in new forms beyond what I imagined, and *the practical* elements would be incorporated from the many processes I had developed in over 20 years of research, study, and application, synthesizing evolutionary schools of thought into my own methods of simplicity.

The practical methodology was what I had taught in large and small communities, with results that benefited thousands of people from all walks of life. I always believed you should learn from the best, incorporate their expertise, delete what was superfluous to your vision, and add in the cutting-edge knowledge that your own focused path would accelerate; this proved to be a theory that benefited my entrepreneurial life as well, since you are always beginning over, without having to start from the beginning.

the yearning for learning

In my youth I was afraid of just about everything, but in later years when I could learn without fear of being tested – I became a sponge for knowledge. I fell in LOVE with learning! As noted previously, when I found my first teacher of higher education, not in a university, but in the halls of a meditation master where the pain of my past began dissolving alongside recognition of what inner worlds might instill – I delved into ancient scriptural wisdom from Vedic, Hindu, and Sufi traditions, consuming them into my Christian upbringing in the way you might devour a delectable new dessert. I wasn't interested in being a scholar, but in *experiencing* the wisdom – and for 11 years I traveled the globe apprenticing; learning, living, loving, and growing.

Being in the apprenticeship of an enlightened teacher, like Gurumayi, was for me similar to stories of old, where matter is converted into gold through a process of alchemy; the fires of my education burned away so much unconscious behavior. Yes, an amazing gift to receive – and one that could be enormously uncomfortable, as facing our frailty always is. Yet what I wanted more than anything was to experience the love and peace all teachers in service of the Truth espouse.

As more doors of education flew open, I was led to a variety of alternative forms of healing and studied the ancient discipline of Jin Shin Jyutsu, where life energy flows in the body, once redirected to be in their natural rhythm with universal energy, support and bring your overall health into harmony. What I absorbed through the master was an example of living the wisdom she taught, and then through my own experiences and study for more than 15 years, I understood how our health profoundly correlates to what we think and believe, i.e., what makes our physiology function.

the practical… awesome education

After years of service and studying ancient teachings, it was now time to get back into the professional world. My husband always had to laugh whenever he got in my car; tapes were everywhere – not the usual rocking-out driving music you might expect, but every new seminar I thought would broaden my mind. Among the very best were Stephen Covey's value-driven *The 7 Habits of Highly Effective People*[1], Neuro Linguistic Programing[2], Warren Bennis[3] and other experts on leadership and communication, the eminently fearless Tony Robbins[4] interviewing brilliant innovative minds like his, Abraham-Hicks[5] expansive and fun approach to the laws of attraction, Dr

Deepak Chopra's[6] unprecedented scientific findings on health and healing, and spiritual chanting when it was time for the mind to rest.

My sweet talk in those days was often more along the lines of, "Honey, honey, just listen to THIS!!!" My enthusiasm would prevail, but usually after 20 to 30 minutes, my normally agreeable husband would emphatically state that he'd had enough *learning* and just needed to chill.

entering the professional world with a new bag of tricks
When I chaired a committee for a non-profit organization and became a national director for another, guiding large communities of people, I wanted to learn more about leadership. I wasn't interested in being in charge; I was passionate about inspiring people to move toward a common vision. The diverse education I had received and applied through years of first-hand experience was now synthesized into simple and practical methods implemented by thousands of people. One particular indebted community reached an extraordinary level of prosperity and financial gain, demonstrated by each individual's accelerated growth in their personal worth, which ultimately allowed them to purchase a multimillion-dollar community center.

My life had become infused by the benefits of a passion that instigated a creative force of constant curiosity and fulfillment. My only concern was that I might run out of remarkable things to learn and share. When I found something I loved, I focused on it with intensity. When I got how I could take responsibility for my life and create it to be one of my dreams, I incorporated whatever study and research was most appropriate, developing processes where envisioning was intentional and taking action was focused. I became partner in a design firm where my newly devised methods presented opportunities; clients would suddenly appear with unlimited budgets, along with purchasing trips to Paris, Puerto Vallarta, New York, and Santa Fe. Dream it, journal it, live it.

When I later became a film producer, more circumstances arose to use my simplified methods of incorporating principled leadership with spiritual values of service and the universal laws of attraction. Creating what I envisioned through these unusual processes assisted my partner and me in ways no one could believe. We produced an award-winning film my first year in the industry, which, if you know anything about Hollywood, is a very unusual occurrence.

when breakdowns lead to life-altering breakthroughs

And then the injury appeared that caused me to return to my true quest – to experience that boundless Love I had read about in the texts and poetry of those who knew it well. *Making Requests* was a practice I developed, combining the humility and eloquence of prayer with the magnified potency of intention, and I implemented it now to discover what was needed to regain my health.

Within a week a tequila-drinking healer appeared on my doorstep whose insights and abilities broke through layers of misconceptions I didn't even know I had. This ordinary man, with an outlandish personality and generous heart, confirmed my belief that it wasn't only sages and mystics who could access this unbounded Energy stream, we could all connect to our innate gifts when the time was right – and not in some distant future… NOW.

the profound... from knowledge to experience
I became one-pointed in my vision, incorporating the methods of simplicity I had created that I felt would assist me most. I spent time in Stillness almost every day. It was different than previous meditations as a vibrant energy had begun to resonate within me. This depth of Stillness is like a unique form of prayer, where you are not negotiating or pleading for anything, but are *BE-ing* in communion with your highest Truth, receiving and offering unconditional Love. Imagine the energy field you are accessing during this time, and how this could accelerate your highest aspirations.

I made *Requests* consistently and with great humility. This comprehensive approach to combining directed quantum energy potential with ancient spiritual wisdom revealed more than I ever dreamed – in a few months' time, the experience I had longed for – appeared.

Today, research on the benefits of prayer and meditation not previously realized, is giving pause for thought; what else could be possible that hasn't been considered? A recent article by Michael J Formica, MS, MA, EdM in *Psychology Today*[7] reveals an interesting scientific study from Duke University Medical Center:

"... within a group of 150 cardiac patients received alternative post-operative therapy treatment, the sub-group who also received intercessory prayer (they were prayed for) had the highest success rate within the entire cohort. The fascinating thing about the study is that it was double-blind – neither the researchers, nor those on the receiving end of the intercessory prayer knew that these patients were being prayed for – suggesting an intervening variable.

From a metaphysical perspective, what we are talking about here is the reciprocal resonance that has been demonstrated to exist between states of consciousness – specifically, casual states of consciousness (prayer, meditation and deep, dreamless sleep) – and the quantum field (what we like to call reality) described by quantum physics.

From a more practical perspective, the notion of this relationship leads us to consider both the individual and collective experience of prayer, and the potential influence it can have on our experience both in and of the world."

The Practices I had initiated resonated through that quantum field, inviting this life-altering experience of absolute peace. I discovered over time that subtler levels could be accessed readily, and would connect me to a transcendent calm where depths of wisdom brought unimaginable inspiration. Stillness was the vehicle, and the rocket fuel powering it was that universal Energy stream. Now it was time to find a way to incorporate it into the day-to-day practicalities of life.

integrating the profound into the practical
Reflecting on the knowledge learned, experiential as well as spiritual, intellectual, and scientific, inspired me to create more practices for transforming my insensitive traits into caring qualities, and also to explore how this transformative gift would be exchanged beyond an individual basis. The perfect solutions emerged through consistently atypical circumstances.

When I learned this Energy could be transmitted through sound resonance, Stillness Sessions were developed, *the profound* element of The SOS Method, recordings with music and words that made it possible for anyone, anywhere to tap into this field of infinite potential. These recordings could match the way we live today by using the latest technology – cell phones, computers, and tablets to bring the inward experience to each person in a way that suits their lifestyle. Stillness Sessions brought benefits to individuals around the globe, comparable to the many scientific reports on meditation:

" 'The Benefits of Meditation', an article authored by Mayo Clinic doctors states, 'Meditation can give you a sense of calm, peace and balance that benefits both your emotional well-being and your overall health. And these benefits don't end when your meditation session ends. Meditation can help carry you more calmly through your day and can even improve certain medical conditions.

Meditation and emotional well-being: When you meditate, you clear away the information overload that build up every day and contributes to your stress. The emotional benefits of meditation include: Gaining a new perspective on stressful situations, building skills to manage your stress, increasing self-awareness, focusing on the present, and reducing negative emotions. [8]

'The Science of Meditation' by Cary Barbor, in *Psychology Today*,[9] 'A second study published last year in *Psychosomatic Medicine*, taught a randomized group of 90 cancer patients mindful meditation (another type of practice). After seven weeks, those who had meditated reported that they were significantly less depressed, anxious, angry and confused than the control group which hadn't practiced meditation."

Since researchers like Herbert Benson MD, founder of the Mind/ Body Institute at Massachusetts General Hospital in Boston, Andrew Newberg MD, and Mark Waldman of the University of Pennsylvania's Center for Spirituality and the Mind began amassing data, many studies have shown that meditation has not only a mental, but also a profound physiological effect on the body.

Meditation offers extraordinary benefits that substantially improve the quality of our lives and our health – so, why aren't more people doing it? Many people feel they just don't have the 30 or even 20 minutes a day that some meditation techniques require; while many practice various types of meditation successfully, a larger segment of society have tried, found it *boring* or impossible to *quiet the mind* and instead have chosen other *recreational* pastimes that are often extremely detrimental to their health.

keeping it so, so simple... yet so, so transformational

With Stillness Sessions there is nothing to repeat, nothing to visualize. By simply listening to recordings infused with this infinite intelligence, some as brief as 11 minutes, a new perception of life opens, where stress disappears and feelings of love expand. People consistently attest to the simplicity with a bit of wonder – how can something this effortless be so effective? How can it touch people so deeply that heart-to-heart connection happens spontaneously, where deep and lasting friendships are made; even people with *apparent* cultural differences? A young woman who's been practicing The Simplicity of Stillness for the last seven years had an answer:

"I have always had a tough time hanging onto painful stories and memories, trying to bury them and pretend that they are no longer a part of my current reality... but the truth is, it's nice to look back and see how far I've come.

Just a few days ago, I broke off a 3+ year relationship and, upon reflection, realized that I don't regret even a moment of it. I have never opened up or shared so much of my true self with a person before – and I realized it's okay to let go because I know who I am and I am HAPPY with who I am. Break-ups are so much easier when there is no hostility, resentment, anger, etc.

Before he moved his last boxes out, he said, 'I will forever remember you for how beautiful you thought the world was and for how much love you poured into it.' That was a fantastic moment for me... looking back on how angry I used to be and how much negativity I sent out... and now I am seen as someone who sends love into the world? Amazing.

If I had these tools from a very young age and understood how to use them and why they were important... had parents who guided me... I wonder how different life could have been. Imagine an ENTIRE lifetime of peace... sounds pretty good to me..."

We are all vehicles for bringing this loving Energy of peace into the world. We are all students, and teachers – learning, living, and growing together. It is my wish and highest intention that The Simplicity of Stillness Method ignites the power in you to consistently recognize your innate brilliance. Once you say yes, that Love will grow boundlessly. It really is that simple. Follow the steps outlined in this book... and just keep saying yes.

A FEW BASIC PRINCIPLES

Within the pages of this book you'll find a simple method for connecting with the power of peace in you. It is not an idea or a mental construct of adding knowledge to the library of your mind – it is *experiential* and you recognize it through the natural metamorphosis of your life choices, habits, and actions.

What this illuminating methodology accesses – improves and transforms the quality of your life in every moment.

When your perception of life changes, so does the world around you. You become more adept at handling challenges, managing health and wealth, making choices that express your values, and creating dreams that match your aspirations to live a meaningful life.

When the mind can grasp what is possible, it will support our experiential journey into new worlds; therefore I have included many references from scientists and accomplished professionals throughout the book to offer your mind this knowledge in greater detail. The seven fundamental principles in this book are:

- Everything in the universe consists of Energy – human beings are Energy in form. (The capital *E* is used to clarify that this Energy *is not* what we recognize in coffee, caffeinated drinks, or one's personality.)

- This Energy is the life force that sustains and maintains our world, and is given different names depending on our understanding. Whether we find it in nature, or name it God, infinite intelligence, source, or the quantum field – at the core it is all the same.

- Science informs us that a field of universal intelligence surrounds us, but neglects to explain how to access it. What The Simplicity of Stillness Method ignites is a way to connect with this conscious Energy stream and live from the awareness accessed.

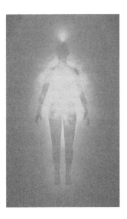

ENERGY
The Life-force Energy in You

- Human beings vibrate at different frequencies; the Energy field of consciousness, light, and peace is a high vibration[1] that can be integrated into our denser bodies naturally over time.

- As this power moves through you in greater measurement, that electromagnetic field, the higher vibrations of consciousness emanate, benefiting and uplifting those around you – ultimately including extensive circles of influence.

- Humanity's natural progression, from the lower frequencies of survival to higher consciousness, is evolving more rapidly now so that we can become a more enlightened society, valuing each person and caring for this earth.

- When you're ready to broaden your horizons and accept the gifts you're capable of, life's mysteries begin to unravel.

This is not about receiving anything outside of you, but is an acceleration of the innate power within.

The meaning of *power* in this book is: That which supports the significance of life itself. This is not associated with *force*, which creates counterforce, effecting polarization over unification. Power in contrast '… appeals to what uplifts, dignifies, and ennobles'.[2]

The Energy of peace resonating through the Stillness Session audio accompanying this book is one way to ignite that innate power. Regardless of culture, age, or background, the experience this methodology offers invites benefits into your life – beginning with knowing tranquility in your heart.

orchestrating the quantum soup
Different ways we attune to this timeless intelligence are through sound, sight, touch, and intention:

Sound: Conscious awareness resonates through sound. When you listen to something that holds higher frequencies, such as Tibetan bowls[3], or the resonance of a sacred chant, it's possible to tap into that unified field unrestricted by time or space. 'The fact that the human body… exchanged information with a *mutable field*… suggested something profound about the world. It hinted at human capabilities for knowledge and communication far deeper and more extended than we presently understand…'[4]

The words and music in Stillness Sessions transmit a level of vibrational communication that transcends time and space. Numerous scientific reports describe how it's possible for virtual events to affect the physical world. In simple terms, what is being revealed is how it's possible for this *field of information* – the quantum soup that the universe and we exist in – to orchestrate activity that can occur instantly regardless of time or distance. This is another way of explaining why it's possible to have life-altering occurrences, purely by listening to .audio infused with the power of infinite presence.

Around the world countless people's lives have been transformed by listening to this uniquely different fusion of meditation, prayer, and that heightened Energy stream. Many report a surge of love in their hearts, as impurities expel past pain that has been trapped in their unconscious. Awareness expands exponentially, demonstrating what science and ancient wisdom have told us – it's not ever about *a physical form,* it's about the *informed field – by whatever name you give it,* and each of us can choose (or not) to engage in this exchange.

Sight: Reading and reflecting on passages in a book written from that limitless dimension connects us to the deep spaciousness within the words, and to that sacred presence in us. When we ask for the light of consciousness to bring us true knowledge, it becomes the determining factor that irrigates our souls with the still waters of illumination. Suddenly we can see what has been right before our eyes, shielded only by a haze of unconscious thinking. Quite naturally, lifetimes of blockage are released – and we are inspired to act in a way that propels synchronistic events into our lives. We find ourselves in this undeniably distinctive *flow of life*.

Touch: Throughout time, hands have represented blessings streaming into the world; a reservoir of sensorial force, an extension of power and strength. Many people speak of a tingling sensation that occurs as the igniting power of this Energy is expressed through a variety of means, including touch. This *vibration* felt in the hands, as well as throughout the entire body, taught me who we are, beyond the physical, beyond the images we create when we don't have knowledge of the formless nature of our soul. Touch is another way this dimension communicates to and through us to offer Love to this world.

Intention: The very fabric of this universe is matter and energy – and *matter* (atoms and molecules) consists of energy. Thoughts are a form of energy, and can bring events into reality through intention, the concentration of our attention. When you consider that all actions are created first by thought, it becomes clear how much our thoughts participate in creating our lives. The practices in this book support new thoughts that align with your vision of where you want to focus your attention.

George Bernard Shaw expressed it this way: 'Some men see things as they are and ask why? I dream things that never were and ask why not?' This visionary instinctively knew the power of intention to create life beyond the boundaries of what he could see. As focused thought is sent into a quantum field it has the organizing power to bring fulfillment. Then all that's left to do is walk the journey, keep it simple, and allow the eternalness of you to live the greatest adventure you can dream.

THE SIMPLICITY OF STILLNESS METHOD DEFINED

the convergence of the creative with the logical...
the heart with the mind

The Simplicity of Stillness is a method for higher learning that converges intellectual knowledge with *experiential* wisdom. This stunningly simple process ignites and expands the power of peace in you, dramatically transforming your experience of life.

Often described as the antidote to life's greatest challenges, from addiction to depression – connection to this Energy of infinite intelligence releases the stress and anxiety caused by life's uncertainty and expands hope, healing and happiness into every day.

This experiential teaching method synthesizes research, study, and application from ancient meditation traditions, healing disciplines, evolutionary schools of thought, with the life force Energy that informs all of the Simplicity of Stillness work.

1. **Stillness Sessions** are a new form of meditation, infused with *(the profound)* Energy of pure peace. Simply listening to the words and music ignites a journey of greater awareness.

2. **The Three Breath Awareness** is a reconnection tool for accessing this state of peace and inspiration in moments.

3. **The SOS Practices** *(the practical)* are processes for integrating infinite intelligence into daily life.

THE CONVERGENCE OF THE CREATIVE WITH THE LOGICAL, THE HEART WITH THE MIND

You can't *choose* new behaviors if you aren't *aware* that your actions are causing the pain you are experiencing. Since your life choices, habits, behaviors, and actions create your life circumstances, it's important to develop a capacity for shaping new beliefs.

An *experiential* connection to infinite intelligence accelerates the process. You guide the momentum and *speed* of your journey through your intention and commitment. The knowledge you find informs and supports your heart/mind connection.

This simple form of learning ultimately leads to living at your highest potential: an empowered fulfilling life.

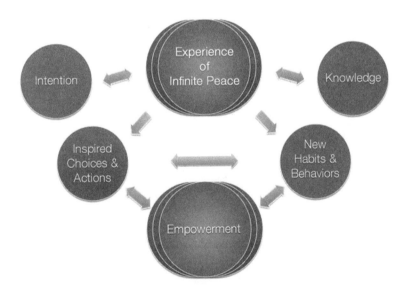

HOW TO USE THIS BOOK

Ask any athlete, Olympian, or musician what it takes to run the race, play the game, or perform music in a way that is effortless, where the moves you make flow through you without thought. The answer will undoubtedly be... practice. While each person might have been born with natural talent, it took focus, will, intention, and practice to be at the top of their game. The good news is, in this *game*, you begin with innate talent, so even if it's been hidden, you now have access to a fathomless reservoir of human potential.

Every person's journey is perfect in its evolution and brings a greater confidence that life can be just as extraordinary as we dare to dream. *The Power of Peace in You* is meant to assist you each time you pick it up, as it is layered with *reflective thoughts* and poems, inviting you to become still and breathe... slowing down your pace... to find that rhythm where you can enjoy each moment, even those that might challenge you today.

Some of you will have wondrous experiences immediately as you connect to the essence of peace flowing through the words, or in the Stillness Session CD. As we now know, time and distance are inconsequential. Some of you will have feelings of deep tranquility and tenderness as your heart recognizes its connection to limitless Love.

And some of you might question if anything is happening – until a week or a month from now when you notice that something has shifted. *Life is not the same.* The happiness you feel is deeper. Your body feels more in tune. The exhaustion you lived with for years has dissipated, and what remains is a lightness of being that gives you a different perspective on life. This process develops through your life experiences, and will unfold through a progression of time. It has the power to rescript unconscious thinking. Each week's practice creates the perfect structure for dissolving unresouceful beliefs and constrictive patterns. Sometimes it could feel like your world is turning upside down, and in some sense, it is. Forming new habits is never simple. As you integrate this higher vibration of peace into your life, it will calm the mind and ease your transitions.

Does this mean we will no longer have any troubles to deal with? Will the contaminated rivers of this world suddenly become clean and the heavens pour rain down on all the parched lands? Maybe – but more likely, these are the *concepts* that need to be released so we can actually become aware of the amazing new paradigms that *are* being revealed.

This is about embracing the full measure of you and your aspirations, where you are participating in the development of the person that creates the life and the world you wish to live in. Everything you will ever need for recognizing true freedom exists within you in this very moment – the odyssey itself will become your greatest teacher.

There are numerous ways to read this book. Reading sequentially is an excellent idea, as reviewing *Laying The Foundation* before getting into the stories will clarify how these unusual events could occur, and will prepare you for all that is about to open in your own life.

Or, you can read it slowly over time, finding the chapter that is most important to where you are in your life, absorbing the teaching, following the practice outlined, and integrating the experience into your life. Then return to absorb another teaching and practice the following week.

What absolute peace offers us – is life altering; it transforms the human condition into a new sphere of awareness where change is not only imminent and possible, it is probable. And it happens so simply… by connecting with the limitless stream of consciousness that is here now to show us the way.

THE PURPOSE OF THIS BOOK
You can't create lasting peace in the world until you find it in your own heart. ~ Marlise

There has never been a time like this when ideas can circle the planet in a matter of minutes; when we can access an experience of our essential nature – and through our interrelatedness share that magnification across every apparent cultural divide. *The Power of Peace in You* is a transformational tool to assist an awakening of great magnitude, where we can shift from the elemental patterns of our ancestry of shame, guilt, apathy, fear, and anger into higher frequencies of consciousness corresponding with acceptance, reason, willingness, love, and peace.

This evolutionary time marks a crossroad where humanity has the opportunity to evolve rapidly beyond the incremental shifts that have brought us from the survival mode of the hunter-gatherers to a future that has the promise of the unimagined. Massive technological achievements where humankind can interact with one another on a global level are now defining unprecedented possibilities.

I was fortunate to hear lectures given by Don Johanson[1], the paleoanthropologist who established The Institute of Human Origins, where he spoke of humanity ever-so-slowly evolving – into a consciousness that could create today's technology. He considers the leap in evolution from the Neanderthal to the next stage as having occurred when they began trading with one another – in other words, when they had found a way to '... *be in communication*'. And isn't that what is so uniquely special about the 21st century where we are *interacting* with one another globally as never before?

In *Power vs. Force*, Dr David R Hawkins reviews the stages humanity passes through in our evolution.[2] The 29-year study he describes is especially insightful regarding the energetic frequencies of human behavior. In this and later books he explains the transitions from an ego-dominated life based on survival to progressive conscious awareness, and having a greater capacity for love through the non-linear evolution of the *energy of life* itself.

evolutionary energy... revolutionary time...
don't you know it's gonna be all right

The timing of a new dimension of consciousness opening, which has not been accessible to the masses until now, promises profound effects beyond what most of us can even imagine, where more people can develop advanced levels of awareness that will set a precedent for how human beings interact with one another in centuries to come. Science has discovered evidence that our brain is not finite; we are capable of behaving in ways that recognize our shared humanity and the intrinsic interconnectedness we have with each other, regardless of cultural, generational, or economic differences. We *can* turn challenges into opportunities, diminish suffering, and increase our enjoyment of life, so that even the simplest moments are filled with appreciation and purpose.

For those ready to explore the unknown inner worlds presented to us today through the lens of this accessible field of awareness being birthed, they will find that it is not solely about time spent in solitary meditation. It's about a new way of living: bringing that *Energy of life* into the now, rising above separation, *BE-ing with each other*, standing together in recognition of our global connectedness to create solutions for this planet – to not only survive the colossal challenges ahead but to thrive and create a new prosperity out of the innate genius we can now access.

choices based on heart/mind coherence...

Love is not intellectual, it emanates from the heart; living separate from this way of BE-ing and relating to the world will no longer be a viable option. Those who cling to old structures will find there is nothing to hold onto as outdated constructs collapse. Economies will continue to fall, as they have; governments will topple, as we've seen; and people who have not learned to live in alignment with their heart will be helplessly lost as relationships thought to be fulfilling no longer have meaning. From political leadership to close personal ties, we will witness the dissolution of humanity's mindless ambitions and endless discord and conflict; what is arising is being replaced with higher levels of courage, well-being, and self-expression.

The ultimate purpose of The Simplicity of Stillness Method is to ignite and expand the power of infinite peace within so that we can discover, and learn to create outer expressions of the inner peace and purpose that is our innate heritage. The most respected visionaries of every age have told us that every person has this inherent greatness within them. This universal and at the same time unique *inner knowing* yearns for us to consciously choose to let it communicate with and through us. So, what would that look like? For some it will be a way to dream the impossible dream and see it unfold; for others it will be to live life simply, surrounded by love and filled with the contentment of a life well lived.

from noise to equipoise

In a world where our mind is often cluttered with vast amounts of information, distractions, and complexity, we can easily lose our way. We forget that what ultimately brings us the most happiness is living with purpose, knowing that feeling of complete contentment where nothing needs to be added for life to be great. When we tap into this current of conscious Energy, we tap into limitless inspiration, timeless information, and Love. Our perception of life changes to one that we enjoy more than any limiting belief that has ever held us in its grip. Love, wisdom, courage, and healing are experientially available now for anyone who intends to know it deeply for themselves.

This unique time we are living in has the potential of every dream known to history's most revered leaders, sages, poets, and philosophers. Do we have the courage to enclothe a new form of humanity that is truly the essence of what we once knew, and emerge as the unique and causal agents of a new era? It *is* possible to discover what has been beyond reach for millennia – and what better time than now for it to be revealed.

WHATEVER STEALS YOUR CANDY

Energy, God, Universe, Source, Buddha, Allah, meditation, stillness. Words create pictures where beliefs and judgments of what we like and dislike show up. They can steal our candy from us if we let them. In this book you will find many references to what keeps this universe in motion, who you speak or pray to in the quiet of night, or whatever you consider to be worthy of being referenced as the highest source. You will find words like infinite consciousness, awareness, pure presence, the quantum field, and essence. They are interchangeable. Anytime you see or hear one – and a wall goes up – simply replace it with one of your choice.

A few more *words about words* are included here, to assist you in noticing their effect and hopefully to prevent them from distracting you from your primary intent.

words can steal our candy before we even get to taste it

Words are letters on a page, syllables in someone's mouth that have no meaning until we assign it to them. They are powerful attractors, *and* can produce the opposite effect as well. Words can steal our candy from us if we let them. The word *meditate* used to remind me of time spent waiting for something to happen, even though what this unassuming word represents has benefited countless persons throughout history. Thoughts would appear like, *it's boring, I don't have time, etc.*

I was drawn into Stillness very naturally when I experienced a loving and energized intelligence moving through me; from that moment my life began to change exponentially. Even if my mind chattered, although it rarely did, I always felt sensations of peace come over me. This was unknown territory for someone who lived their life mostly at warp speed, and it was a welcome relief to my entire system that rarely took time to 'smell the roses'.

Sometimes I felt like I was being bathed in the brilliant light of a million suns and it would energize me in an entirely different way than I had known. Time spent in Stillness was a paradox of serenity and electrifying excitement. It created a will within me to return to it again and again. The essential point here is – words can be like the pulsation of life itself, entraining and inviting us to travel uncharted territory, or they can be like thieves who have come to steal our candy in the night. You get to choose which road you will travel – you just want to notice if you are making that choice, or if a 'concept' you have is taking it away from you.

delectable, delicious, divine candy...
As you become aware of the power of language to draw circumstances and events into your life, notice any words that could steal happiness from you, and replace them with those of your choice. Choose words that light you up. Create new ones if you want, but choose a vocabulary that allows you to discover the treasures beyond the words.

Become more conscious of what you speak, write, and think. Find a language of words that inspire you, that shape the world to be one that you dream, not those that make you want to pull the covers over your head and go back to sleep. Allow this simple awareness to offer you the most delectable candy available and feel free to enjoy as much as you want.

THE PRACTICE

CONTEMPLATION & JOURNALING
retrieving illuminated knowledge beyond our
everyday understanding

Contemplation & Journaling is a core practice of The Simplicity of Stillness Method. I invite you to experiment with it as you journey through this book. You could find it so enriching, it will become a habit you can't live without. I've been doing it for years. Why? It works.

The Practice of Contemplation & Journaling was designed to complement your experience of Stillness, to assist in deepening your awareness of your Self and bring fresh insight and understanding to your life experience. It illuminates what you think you know and what you don't, in ways that are not possible by any other means. *Journaling grounds inspired thoughts and insights and brings them to reality* – without it so much would be lost, similar to *aha* moments that dissipate if they're not integrated into life.

As the Energy field of peace begins to magnify your awareness, guidance comes in many forms. Contemplation & Journaling provides the opportunity to turn your gaze inward, to get clarity from the innate wisdom you have when accessing the source of all knowledge. Most people spend their entire lives looking for answers outside themselves. When you reflect on your life's events, you access greater clarity to become congruent with what you value.

Journaling gives you a record of your development, which gifts you the ability to trust more. I have often reviewed my journal, finding inspirational thoughts that became actual events, challenges that no longer exist, bad habits that disappeared, and dreams that came true. Through the practice of Contemplation & Journaling you can:

- Connect with that deep well of inspiration just waiting to be called upon.
- Experience greater levels of peace, love, compassion,

confidence, and health in your daily life as new levels of wisdom arise to guide you.

- Resolve limitations that may be holding you back from living a life of meaning and passion.
- Reveal guidance of what the next step is in your life journey.
- Become present to the natural gifts, talents, and abilities you've been given to live your inner purpose.

How to Do The Contemplation & Journaling Practice

Contemplation & Journaling is a personal pursuit; the initial goal is simply to find what works for you. The following guidelines are suggestions to help you get started:

- **Find a quiet space** where you won't be interrupted – at home, at the park, or even in a quiet corner of your favorite cafe.
- **Be specific** about what you want to contemplate. It could be a challenge you are facing, or a dream you would like to bring into greater focus.
- **Become still,** close your eyes, do The Three Breath Awareness and reconnect to that knowing within. You can also listen to a Stillness Session CD where that Energy field of unlimited information is transmitted. **Allow the thought to just be in the space**.
- **Listen for ideas and answers** to what you are contemplating. When you get an insight or clarity on a solution, open your eyes and write it down.
- **Continue the contemplation** by simply being aware of the messages filtering through your consciousness in the coming days. The most amazing insights often appear in unexpected forms: phone calls, words in a book, billboards, or what is spoken in a film. Be sure to write insights in your journal.

- **Make a regular commitment** to contemplate and journal your hopes, dreams, and intentions as well as what you would like assistance to release – i.e. old patterns and beliefs. It only takes 5 to 15 minutes, which you might choose to do 3 to 4 times a week. The benefits you'll see are immeasurable.

There are many elements within this book – stories, teachings, contemplative poetry, where you could feel drawn to go deeper into the understanding being revealed. Take The Practice of Contemplation & Journaling and make it your own. Many people, who previously never thought about or wanted to journal, found their beliefs changing while applying this practice into their lives. Many noticed that whatever they wrote in their journal actually began happening. Seeing is believing in this instance, and writing your thoughts is a way to ground them in a reality you won't be able to deny.

This Week's Practice:

Choose to actively participate in your life's journey by contemplating one challenge you'd like to see transformed. Consider how great it would be if you no longer had to deal with it. Write about it in your journal and then follow the instructions written in The Practice above.

Make a commitment to contemplate and journal at least two or three times a week, recording your insights, challenges, and dreams. As you move through each chapter, you will find more and more insights coming your way, revealing what you want to know. Be sure to write them down. What you find might encourage you to make this a lifelong practice, one that will continually stream benefits into your very extraordinary life.

4
THE JOURNEY

HEALING

Healing Blockages, Establishing New Beliefs

Without even realizing it we accept beliefs from society, past circumstances, and well-meaning friends and parents, rarely questioning their authenticity – and these become the self-imposed limitations that direct our actions and choices.

With the expansive awareness that conscious Energy ignites, we can see these blockages, often for the first time. We can then *choose* to release the constrictive habits and layers of resistance that cause so much physiological and psychological pain – and discover the health, power, and freedom that is our true nature. Establishing new beliefs opens gateways of limitless growth and transformation.

INTEGRATION
Acquiring Empowered Habits, Behaviors & Actions

You can't *choose* new behaviors if you aren't *aware* that your actions are causing the pain you're experiencing. Since your life choices, habits, behaviors, and actions create your life circumstances, it's important to develop a capacity for shaping empowering beliefs. Conscious awareness ignites and inspires new beginnings through the choices that are now available to you as your connection to that field of universal intelligence grows.

EMPOWERMENT
Consistent Inspired Choices Reflect Quality of Life

More time is now spent in the up curve than the down; you are Be-ing in the flow of life where synchronicity occurs. Consistent connection to infinite intelligence has transformed the choices you make. You manage life events in a way that grants you a greater quality of life; self-expression, well-being, creativity, and purpose.

The trajectory of conscious awareness accelerates at ever-higher levels, consistent with your commitment to the practices that invite continual expansion and renewal. Your life is a reflection of the person you are and are becoming.

LIFE CIRCUMSTANCES

OVERVIEW: There are 11 Simplicity of Stillness Practices in this book. In Part 4, 'The Journey', each chapter contains a practice that reveals and develops greater **Healing, Integration, and Empowerment**. Conscious choices and the repetition of newly acquired habits develop empowered actions and behavior that generates new life circumstances bringing an exceptional sense of purpose and joy to your daily life.

SUGGESTION: Add Stillness Sessions to your existing [meditation] practices three times a week to begin, and include one SOS Practice as a home study (less than 15 minutes). You will notice the benefits arriving quite rapidly. By the end of the final chapter (used as a 9-week study), you could discover that the extraordinary life you now lead is the one you knew was always waiting to be revealed…

The benefits this process evidences happen naturally over time. Enjoy adding this simple methodology to your life in whatever way serves you best.

stillness is not about sitting in silence 24 seven
it's not about going to the desert or islands
or anywhere you think you can get away from it all

as your connection to the innate power of peace within
deepens - your perception of life shifts

you find calm where others find challenges
you're playing a new note
one that resonates with the flow of life

your perception of the way it is - shifts the way it is
and soon you notice, that whatever way it is
is really ok

it's so ok that one day, looking back, you realize
your suffering has diminished

this is lasting peace that lives out loud...
as well... as in the silence

CHAPTER 1

SOMETHING'S CHANGING...
ARE YOU LISTENING?

reasons are of little consequence,
when a journey of great import resounds...

Every great journey begins with a calling. Some might describe it as a heart impulse, the soul's yearning, or just a longing for something to be different than it is. This quest can be a *knowing* that it's time for even greater expansion of the journey you are already on, or it can appear as a major life challenge such as illness, divorce, or critical financial concerns. Whether you are conscious of the reason isn't important. And, it's possibly why this book has found its way to you now...

The world we live in is changing. The demands of our 21st-century lives, makes it appear difficult to escape or shift what impacts us all; unprecedented economic pressures, job cuts and losses, rising health costs, warfare, and environmental destruction, along with numerous other crises. However, in the midst of this uncertainty, an evolved awareness has been birthed.

letting go of the status quo
The arising consciousness is a movement away from the social conditions of a world where fear, greed, secrecy, manipulation, control, and self-interest at others expense exist – toward a more loving, compassionate, and sustainable world. Movement, momentum, energy in motion – are all key elements propelling

people globally to new levels of engagement – reawakening the understanding that it's time to reclaim our natural power and live connected to the infinite *Energy* we truly are.

What if change meant life could become simpler, more gratifying, more enlightening? The Renaissance was a time of unfathomable progress that occurred over a span of hundreds of years. In this age of stunning technological development, why wouldn't there also be the emergence of new methodologies to pioneer the inner worlds as never before? The next evolution of the human spirit is happening in a lot less time. The transition is already underway.

To proceed on a journey of transformation, a willingness to let go of the status quo is essential. We often battle to keep things they way they are, even if we're unhappy. But what if reclaiming our natural power was a graceful unfolding? What if we are embarking on a new world of possibilities that will only become apparent once we let go of the illusionary safety of what we have always known? What *you* are about to rediscover is a way of living and being that very few people have known before this time, the wonder of a *realized* life. This could be the next step in a longtime evolutionary journey, as it was for me, or it may be your first foray into a new way of living.

heeding the call

That call for me came disguised as an injury. My right hip began to hurt one day, seemingly out of the blue. I had done nothing physically to injure it, yet the symptoms got worse day by day: excruciating pain, difficulty walking and sitting. Doctors were telling me I needed to consider back surgery. I had no idea this injury was my invitation to the most adventurous journey of my life.

Whether we are conscious of it or not, when it's time, our soul's deepest prayer is heard. For many people it arrives through the doorway of our greatest challenges: a job loss, a death, an illness, or a major life crisis. In these moments of apparent 'breakdown' we are actually much closer to 'breakthrough' than we realize. Rarely do we consider these ordeals as invitations to discover the innate power that resides within us. But that's exactly what they are. What is required in this time is your willingness to give thought to the unfolding events in your life, to be open to the lessons and guidance they offer, and a vigilance to stay the path.

the only way out is by going deeper within

As the saying goes, *you can run but you just can't hide*. Well, I could barely walk let alone run! At one point I yelled out in agony, beseeching the powers that be: *"I want to climb mountains in Peru...I want to walk the deserts of Africa!! Show me, guide me, what is it I need to know..."* In the midst of this unbearable pain, what was emerging inside me was a burning desire, which I realized was the messenger, sent to remind me of my deepest longing – to know true freedom, and that I had somehow gotten lost along the way. This dire injury was offering me a journey, to discover a deeper connection with that field of higher intelligence.

I made time for Stillness and it wasn't long before the answers I *requested* surfaced. The untapped potential and natural power that resides inside every one of us, waiting to be discovered – was shown to me – and not conceptually, but experientially as it became integrated into the fabric of my life every day.

There will always be unexpected surprises to greet us on

any adventure we take. One of the wonders I encountered was the understanding of our energetic nature. This evolutionary Energy taught me that there are more rivers to cross, mountains to climb, and pathways to maneuver. By connecting with it, I experienced many exquisitely timeless moments that took my breath away, and so many synchronicities that it's impossible to keep track of them. My body healed and within one year's time I no longer had any pain. As this frequency of pure peace transformed my life, it brought with it the answers I had been seeking – even to those questions I didn't know to ask.

This call to adventure is a signal that entices, cajoles, and insists we get on a new road that leads to what our heart has always yearned to know. We can choose to recognize the signals and awaken to all that is possible in this lifetime, or go back to sleep and live in unconsciousness one more round.

the journey is yours for the taking

We all move at a different pace; each step along the way carries such import, you really don't want to rush it. The Simplicity of Stillness Method is like a roadmap and when you hear the call of this adventure within your soul, I urge you to follow it. This chapter focuses on Stillness and how Stillness Sessions can ignite that experiential element of the cohesive learning model. It includes stories of people who evidence the impact this subtle and momentous connection had on their lives. I believe they'll inspire you to see the possibilities available within your own life as well.

At the end of this chapter is a detailed description of Stillness Sessions and The Three Breath Awareness reconnection tool. Feel free to ignite and expand that Energy stream of absolute peace, anytime you feel the calling; allow it to consistently influence the remarkable journey you are on. Anytime, anywhere… all you have to do is…

Lower the Lights… Switch off the World… Listen…

or

simply take 3 deep breaths…
and reconnect to that knowing within

THE MAN WHO WOULD BE MONK

Although Gauguin named his home *The Isles of Inspiration,* I never could have imagined the remarkable developments that would befall me on my oh-so-uncommon sojourn to Polynesia. For quite some time I had been getting numerous internal *messages* that I was to go to Tahiti. So, when a friend mentioned that she knew of a bungalow perched high on a remote hill, owned by a local family, I instantly knew this is where I was meant to go. I wasn't sure *why,* or what I would be doing once I arrived. The only thing I knew for sure – was that I had to go.

On the boat ride to the island, my host let me know he had studied at one time to be a Christian monk, and was inexorably clear in his beliefs. I smiled and wondered why he had chosen this course of conversation. Tamahere later told me that his first thoughts were to prove that this *Stillness stuff* he had read about on my website couldn't be all that I said and that whatever it was, it *certainly* wasn't for him.

My new Polynesian friend informed me that he had been raised with a very strict religious background. I shared with him that people from many religious traditions all over the world felt no conflict whatsoever and actually felt Stillness enhanced their ability to find peace in their daily lives. His response was in perfect measure to all those who resist avenues of any new understanding, and with a smile anchored in that state of mind, he replied, "… maybe it just isn't right for me."

unexpected truths

What exists within Stillness dissolves the many questions that spin and twirl like a top in one's mind. The good news is there is nothing to believe in. When you eat a slice of hot home-made apple pie with vanilla ice cream melting on top, or you drink an ice-cold lemonade on a hot summer's day – do you need to believe it? It's more likely that your personal experience will tell you all you need to know. Once the power of absolute peace within is accessed, the light is on.

And so it was with the man who would be monk when the unexpected and extraordinary appeared in his life. The sleeping titan that lies within us all, awaiting the perfect moment to be revealed, appeared for Tamahere and the two missionaries who accompanied him, while sitting on the deck of my bungalow listening to a Stillness Session. The experience was so tangible, Tamahere didn't want to leave, as though staying would ensure that what he had just discovered would remain, and that he would never return to the *sleep* of the unknowing again.

The power of that mysterious presence began weaving a new adventure into his life – each day he gained insight into greater freedom, and each day whatever blocked this awareness from him – came up to be dissolved.

* * *

One evening Tamahere drove me to catch a boat heading to a neighboring island where I was staying for a period of time. He mentioned that he had a pain in his shoulder and wondered if I could be of help. I heard myself say that the pain *really hurting* him was not in his shoulder, it was *here*. I placed my hand on the lower part of Tamahere's throat and pressed. The words resonated in the car like the deep tones of a bell rung in empty towers, calling out warnings to all who could hear them. When we don't deal with the pain inside, it grows and closes us off from any chance of real joy in our lives.

I didn't know what Tamahere's pain was, but I suddenly had the knowing that he was hurting. Tamahere became silent and so did I. We can allow higher consciousness to move through us and offer knowledge to others when we trust what's there to come through. This was definitely one of those times as I was listening to myself speak words I didn't know were there.

Silence descended again and the wind swaying gently through the palm trees became the only sounds we heard as the car moved slowly along the empty road leading to the dock. The sun's golden hues shimmered brilliantly across the sky, lightly caressing the water on its descent into the horizon. In times of Stillness, our powers of observation increase, allowing us a visual and insightful clarity that opens windows into realities rarely seen. This moment captured that unmistakable beauty. Those who are uncomfortable with silence will miss these precious gifts, while those who recognize the silken pearl that awaits them will find it filled with inspiration.

the soundless hush

You can grow to love the soundless hush within the quiet. It's an acquired taste that grows as you perceive the aliveness within it. The understanding of this perfection arises not through learned patience, but when you fall in love with each moment and are not in any rush to see it go.

Tamahere was about to discover another sort of pearl, a gift offered from the depths of the sea of unconsciousness. His new awareness encouraged him to speak aloud the dark secrets he had kept hidden for so many years. His voice faltered as he spoke, like someone who's taken two steps forward and wants to take them back.

"I haven't told this to anyone... but... when I was a child, I was raised in Catholic schools... my teacher was very strict. One day we were playing hide and seek..." His voice ricocheted like a bullet unable to find its target as the pain within the memory reignited. He remembered racing across the room to hide when somehow he got wrapped beneath the many skirts his teacher was wearing and how it maddened her. "She put me on her desk in front of the entire class... and took off all my clothes... I had to stand there for a very long time... naked... in front of everyone..."

You could feel his pain; the shame he experienced so long ago had not left him. The punishment had scarred Tamahere in ways that weren't obvious to the eye, but the wounds it left were still holding him captive. The memories haunted him. They were beyond the borders of acceptance, and much like the ravages of any acts against humanity, they were the basis for many of the challenges he had been dealing with since he was a child.

The boundless power of his inner knowing brought this incident into consciousness to be transformed. From the very depths, where we keep our innermost secrets, the light recovered it to assure Tamahere he would no longer have to live with this decay eating away at his very core. He was an extraordinary man, filled with compassion and love, and his recognition of this had remained concealed from him throughout his life.

This sleeping giant was awakening now from the slumber of humanity's darkest hours.

Tamahere had studied to be a monk so he could know God's love, the love he was robbed of as a child – but only after the memory from his past came into the Light, could this man whose name actually meant *the loved child* in Tahitian, reacquaint himself with the man he truly was.

the healing power of peace

In the days ahead, the power of peace accelerated his passion for life; that awakening Energy grew within him quite naturally and he continued doing Stillness Sessions to further integrate it. When I saw Tamahere again the deep lines on his face had melted, and a happy, you could even say joyous, man stood there ready to take on the world. Something had shifted. The Light was, literally and figuratively, shining through the dense matter of his physical body and radiating happiness that everyone within a wide radius of him could see. When suffering is released we are shown just how luminous we truly are.

Tamahere and a friend, who had also drawn this awakening experience to him, had let go of many things from their past, including countless disappointments they had never dealt with. They had sat on the end of a dock laughing and crying into the warm windswept nights, sharing stories that released them both from lifetimes of pain. And now, they couldn't stop smiling – and neither could I.

The omnipotent winds of change that blew into Tamahere's life from that time in Stillness reconnected him to the power that was always there inside. Not from a stance of brawn and force but from a core of enduring strength that is far greater – the power of infinite Love. Every time I see their faces in my mind's eye, it brings a smile to my heart. I am so grateful for the *knowing* that guides us to the infinite wisdom beyond the mind. And, if going to Tahiti is one way to learn – I'm always ready to take that ride.

BLONDE, BEAUTIFUL & SO MUCH MORE

Betsy had everything most men want. But what Betsy wanted most – was to speak her own voice, which she didn't easily do. There'd been men in her life who disapproved of attractive women having strong opinions, that old adage still alive in the 21st century – as though it was somehow unacceptable to be both beautiful, strong, and extremely intelligent.

Eventually, Betsy's diminutive voice became so soft-spoken you rarely heard it, and so intimidated, she rarely used it. And so, as is the case with many people – men and women – her talents became unconsciously imprisoned in a fortress of fear. When Betsy would finally gather the courage to speak, her astute and insightful suggestions were sprinkled with constant apologies, *"Excuse me... I'm sorry, but..."* It was sad to see, and still you couldn't help but adore her gentle loving heart.

gifts of awakening

After the loss of her job as an attorney in a prominent Los Angeles firm, Betsy wanted more than ever to find her true voice. What transpired is the stuff of fairy tales, and yet it is available to even the most skeptical when the time is right. This very classic lady who rarely had a hair out of place, or a wrinkle in her designer suit, had an astonishing vision during her first time in Stillness. When she opened her eyes, there was a look of wonderment replacing the timorous pallor that stems from one who has yet to learn of their true heritage.

Tears trickled down her cheeks like the gentle rain that precedes a downpour. Betsy spoke in a whisper of what she had witnessed. "There were so many people sitting all around me. They were dressed in clothes of the different cultures they came from... and each of them had come to teach me something... something special about... me..."

Her whispered voice sweetly trailed through the room where we sat, surrounded by the particles of Stillness that can be palpably experienced when illumined Love is present. Each moment was charged with that timeless Energy resonating in the space. When your heart feels the Love it has longed to know for lifetimes, you never want it to end. Betsy was wrapped in the essence of the knowledge she had been seeking, "... to know the person I truly am..."

Her mother had also appeared in the vision, giving voice to what she couldn't when Betsy was a child. She had never taught her daughter how to believe in herself, as she hadn't found that expression within herself. And she had never spoken the words all children want to hear, how truly proud she was of her daughter. What was revealed in the Stillness allowed Betsy to see her mother's frailties. In that moment, there was forgiveness; the blame she had carried for so long was finally released. Love burst forth in the neglected garden that had become overgrown with weeds of unconscious discontent.

* * *

The once timorous attorney had a different countenance when I saw her a week later. She shared how Stillness had become a great comfort and how she loved listening to the Sessions as she drifted off to sleep at night. Betsy moved with a sense of confidence I hadn't seen before. A mischievous smile verified that much in her life had changed, and with a nod of recognition she told me about the uncommon week she had. When an overbearing man commandeered the conversation at an annual couple's dinner, Betsy responded in a uniquely different and rather bold manner, voicing her thoughts aloud, "Do any of you have something more to add? It would be so nice if we could hear from *all of you* ... as well."

The room became very quiet. Something had shifted, a new energy had opened in the space, and soon emboldened conversations were popping up everywhere. Voices were heard that usually weren't. The evening was so enjoyable numerous guests thanked her personally. Betsy's husband looked at her glowing face with the astonishment of one who has seen a race horse win, after years of showing in the bottom five, and inquired with wide-eyed confusion, "What has come over you, Betsy? *Who are you??*"

* * *

Each week as years of pent-up fear, anxiousness, and feelings of cowardliness left her, newfound strength lined the muscles of her stature. Betsy found a new love for life surfacing. "I never knew what I wanted before; everything looked so big, so monumental. Now it's easy for me to identify. Nothing's that big; *it's just the next step."* I had to laugh as I wanted to repeat her husband's proclamations myself, but I couldn't get a word in. Betsy's enthusiasm kept pouring out, "I feel like I am finally the captain of my own ship!"

Well, that ship was definitely in safe harbor. Talk about a change in perspective! Betsy was being who she always wanted to be: *herself*, a gracious tower of strength. Stillness became a regular part of her life; her inner guidance expanded and set her free. This sleeping beauty was ready to fulfill her dreams.

angels and attorneys

Two months later Betsy landed a new job at one of the most prestigious law firms in Los Angeles. Three months after that, they promoted her to managing partner! It was then this vibrant, intelligent blonde got the dream that had been written on her heart for years – to be second chair in a jury trial. On the day she was called to represent her client in court, she was serenely fearless. After speaking on his behalf to the jury, her client looked at her with appreciation and disbelief. Inquiring with absolute sincerity, he spoke the words she had become accustomed to hearing, "*Who are you??*" followed by new ones she had never heard before, "Are you an angel??"

We don't often consider *angels* and *attorneys* as two words that are descriptive of each other, but I imagine Betsy could change our opinion. The voice she always wanted – brought these two *worlds together*, and I doubt they'll ever be separate again – as long as Betsy is around.

Finding the courage to speak doesn't come from a false bravado... it resonates from a place of clarity and strength. What is it that you could communicate that would transform your world?

• Listen to the Stillness Session recording.
• Write three insights that could empower you, and take action.

SHANTY TOWN TRANSCENDENCE

You could see how the light had dimmed from their eyes and faces. Some of their struggles were those we've never had to deal with in the Western world, while others were similar – the deep sadness and grief that comes with resignation, discrimination, and hopelessness. Much of the sadness recorded on their dark-skinned faces was from the hardships they endured. Many of these women became wives at the age of 12 or 13. Those who had husbands unable to afford the luxury of more than one wife were left with no support and no way of taking care of themselves or their children.

I arrived at the rural clinic in the middle of the Mara Plains, the home of the Maasai tribe, not knowing what to expect. Their new clinic, with its freshly painted stucco walls and blue-lined windows, stood out like a lone jewel at the edge of a shanty-style town. Talek Village looked like a surreal movie set of one-room buildings with tin siding, no windows, and no plumbing. When you wanted food from the 'store' a man would come running down the mud-packed street, shushing roosters out of the way; from behind the wooden bars above a dust-filled counter he'd ask your bidding.

The previous night had been magical; a Stillness Session brought untold gifts to a tribe of Maasai warriors by the light of a roaring campfire and the glow of an iridescent moon revealed behind storm-laden clouds. The rains had set this unusual occurrence in motion. It was part of a golden thread that was to weave another series of mystical events into my life, and into the world of these disheartened women, just waiting and wanting for life to offer them more than it had.

when the soul's yearning is to know more

Jackson Njapit, the lone practitioner of this last-chance enclave of hope and healing, was among those who discovered the impassioned wisdom in his heart on that extraordinary night. Inspired to share what he had experienced, he invited me to bring 'that blessing of peace' to the women and their babies coming to his clinic the following day.

As I toured the new medical facilities, a warrior appeared: a towering form with chiseled features highlighting skin that was as dark as a moonless sky. If he hadn't been wearing the traditional clothing of the Maasai, he could have stepped out of the pages of *Men's Vogue*. No one knew why he was there, as he wasn't sick. Possibly the whispered talk that echoed through the neighboring villages after last night's unparalleled entrance into new worlds drew him to find out more for himself. Speaking in the English of one who works for the tourist trade, he questioned my background and work. Jackson gently interrupted the warrior's inquiry, informing me before he left on his rounds that the women had gathered and were waiting for me to join them.

Doubtful, skeptical, questioning: *Who is this woman and what could she possibly have to tell me about my life?* I certainly couldn't blame them for being distrustful. These women had every right to be, especially given their backgrounds. More had arrived than Jackson expected, including those who weren't even sick. I wondered what had brought them. We later discovered that some were wives of the men who had been at the session the night before. They had come with that *wanting, that yearning of the soul,* when it's time to rediscover what has been long forgotten.

cultural differences or common ground

Often people believe that our cultural differences mean we have nothing in common, when actually there is a universal ground in our global village. At the hub of it all, beyond any differences, are the values we mutually share in something bigger than ourselves. This understanding was brought into clear view as the inconceivable unfolded before our eyes moment by moment.

A new element was added to the mix of distrustful emotions in the room when a man unexpectedly arrived. As he entered this domain of women he scowled at me from across the room, sending an implicit message of disapproval. He stood glowering above everyone, in striking counterpoint to the women who were positioned below him on a bench that partially circled the room.

There is a long-established Maasai custom that men and women do not fraternize publicly; interestingly, the scowling man did not appear to want to leave. I decided to invite him to stay, only asking that he be seated if he chose to remain. He walked quietly across the room, and *sat down*! I also invited the English-speaking warrior, who had joined us, to participate by translating. He willingly agreed. Something had begun to happen that was outside the cultural norm.

the awakening of tenderness…
the release of intolerant traditions

I spoke about the challenges that all people face and how we all have a deep knowing where we connect to the peace in our hearts. The women appeared curious, while uncertain. I suggested they close their eyes and just feel what this stream of limitless life Energy had to offer them. Unlike the preceding days of tempestuous weather, in this moment, it wasn't raining. The sun was streaming through the windows. The rag-tag curtains billowed as golden light poured through them. The awakening of tenderness could be seen even on the faces of the babies who had all stopped crying and were lying in their mother's arms, eyes open wide, as they drank in the healing ambrosia that pervaded the room.

The warrior seated himself quietly. He caught my eye with a nod indicating a request for this expression of grace to be offered to him in the same way it was being given to the women – through touch. Another set of intolerant traditions began breaking down: the one where men don't sit with women and never allow themselves to be touched in front of them. He was sitting next to a female nurse and yet he opened his mind, his hands, and heart to that honeyed revelation. It radiated throughout the entire clinic in the time of Stillness, and soon you could see people experiencing the wondrous tranquility that had become as thick as heat feels on the open plains.

It's rare to observe a cultural shift this transcendent. And yet, in the company of grace, all barriers disintegrated. Serenity illumined the room. The sorrow and depression that had advanced stress on the faces of the men, women, and children dissolved, and in its place was that glow Love offers us when it permeates our hearts. All hierarchal differences faded into meaninglessness as the nurse, the warrior, women, and children blended into a community that respected the inherent value within each person.

A renowned political leader once stated, when working to create peace in a country whose citizens were intemperate with one another that he wanted to 'make water move uphill'. I don't know if it happened then, but when heightened awareness creates visibility within, this will always be the consequence. Here in Kenya, in a tiny rural clinic, the mists had cleared.

The illuminating diamond waiting to be unearthed in each of us lies just beneath the surface where the beliefs that create human pain are encrusted. These beliefs are set in motion by an unconscious society confirming its universal themes of betrayal, loss, and mortality, assuring the next generation they never forget, unintentionally perpetuating the nightmare. Every one of us has been the recipient of corresponding cultural beliefs. In the way that honing a diamond to perfection is a *process,* we are on training wheels. What awaits us is a jewel of caring and compassion, the recognition of our shared humanity.

I spoke to the now-smiling group about infusing their lives with the Stillness at the source of all inspiration. They could, I promised, lie down in the fields, watch the wheat blowing in the wind, look up into the endless blue of the sky, and touch this Energy of exquisite peace again and again. *Would all their challenges be solved overnight?* No. *Would they shift from where they were?* Yes.

Once we awaken to the essence of our true nature, we see the perfection that exists, and from here, water running uphill is really not a problem...

epilogue

Jackson later relayed to me that many of the villagers' lives were altered from that brief time spent in Stillness. The Maasai female nurse became so accomplished at caring for disabled kids, her services are now required around the world. She has the good fortune of traveling to Italy and other countries where she assists kids who get operations that heal their physical challenges. Many of the tribal women found the strength to create better lives for themselves, and the warrior became one of the most sought-after guides in Kenya, establishing a private company to take care of the many requesting his caring services.

Everything that happened in Jackson Njapit's life requires an entire story to unveil, *Flights of Hope* which you can find in Chapter Four. And, at the end of this chapter is a description of how to bring the Stillness they experienced into your own life, so you can claim that diamond for yourself...

THE PRACTICE

STILLNESS SESSIONS
igniting the inherent power of absolute peace

Everyone wants peace of mind. For billions of people on this planet it is the ultimate wish – and this knowledge, deeply sought throughout history, is no longer a distant dream, it is accessible today as never before. Connecting with the peace, power, and love that is our innate birthright is possible for all people. Everyone reading or hearing these words can ignite this dynamic experiential process for themselves through Stillness Sessions – anytime and anywhere.

Whether you have been on a lifelong journey, or have drawn this experience to you for the first time, you will find the vibrancy of peace magnified in Stillness Sessions igniting a greater understanding of the untapped courage, love, and limitless wisdom in you. This isn't about living separated from life – it's about bringing the principles of our highest values *into* the everyday. Many people who have had moments of illumined clarity can't repeat the experience because they don't fully comprehend what happened or have an idea of how to repeat it. With the advent of the arising consciousness, we can now choose to consistently connect and live at our highest potential.

It is an extraordinary gift to know who we are, beyond the physical that we so often let define us. The expanded reality experience that altered my perception of life taught me that we are all meant to live in this expansive state that enlightens our every choice and action.

Stillness Sessions are an essential element of The Simplicity of Stillness Method where you connect to the innate power at your core, tap into limitless pools of energy and discover how to manage life's challenges with greater ease and inspiration. Simply listening to the music and words, charged with that energetic stream of consciousness, life begins to transform. A heightened capability develops to live from your innate genius[1] as well as a multitude of healing experiences that range from having a greater sense of peace and calm in every day to the awareness needed to heal troubled relationships.

The benefits of meditation are well known. That's why so many people try to make it a daily habit. Unfortunately, many more people have become frustrated as they listen to mindless chatter, watch *to do* lists scroll by in their head, and find they're unable to tap into the clarity, balance, and peace of mind they so desperately want. Whether you have been on a lifelong journey, or have drawn this experience to you for the first time, you will find the vibrancy of peace magnified in Stillness Sessions igniting untapped tranquility, courage, love, and wisdom within you.

The rhythm the Universe dances to – the moon, the tides,

the changing of the seasons all move in accordance with this knowing. Animals don't have clocks or calendars and yet – bears know when to hibernate, birds know when to fly south for the winter, and salmon know when to swim upstream. When you learn to listen to your natural rhythm, you will eat when you are hungry, sleep when you are tired, and move into Stillness when it calls to you.

Once you attune to this universal Energy, it naturally guides your daily decisions, aligning your actions with your true purpose. In this chapter, 'Something's Changing... Are You Listening?' everyone, including Tamahere, Betsy, and the women and men in the clinic in Kenya, discovered a gradual and irreversible shift in their perception of life, some after only one time of connecting to the conscious awareness flowing through Stillness Sessions.

I will be inviting you to return to Stillness consistently throughout the book to continually deepen your connection. My suggestion is to keep it simple; give yourself a bit of alone time, listen to the recording while on a walk, take a few minutes out of your day for a break, try adding it into your morning routine, or just before going to sleep. The rewards are immeasurable *and* pleasurable. Soon, you will be able to experience that connection in the same way so many do today, by just taking a few deep breaths...

Stillness Sessions

- **Find a quiet place, free from interruptions.** Lie down or sit comfortably with your palms open. Close your eyes and relax your body.
- **Listen to the Stillness Session recording** in this book. Follow your breath, and float on the chords of the music. Feel

the tension in your body releasing. Dive into the Stillness at the core of your being.

- **Release all opinions and judgments** of what this moment should look like. Become like a child lying in a field of grass with nothing to do but watch the clouds rolling by...
- **Allow your awareness** to drift beyond time.
- Slowly and gently bring yourself back. **Bring the Energy of peace with you** – feel the difference between where you've been and where you are now. Allow this loving field of awareness to emanate into the space where you are.

Trust in your experience. Whatever you experience is perfect and is what you have drawn to you for the unfolding of your journey of empowerment. Many experience a new depth of peace; some people have visions of the past or future, of brilliant light, as well as physical sensations of tingling, pulsating energy throughout the body. *It's a good idea to write your experiences* in your journal for later reflection, as they will continually change.

This Week's Practice:

- Commit to integrating Stillness Sessions into your life; set how often you'll practice each week. In time you will access this heightened awareness in just a few breaths. Returning to Stillness Sessions will consistently give you an added boost, but you will use them less frequently, as you'll feel the heightened Energy flowing naturally within.
- Create space in your heart and mind to acknowledge that your past can be very different than your future.
- Listen to your deepest knowing. What is truly most important in your life? Follow through on the inspiration given.

- As you move through your day welcome this expansive Energy to guide you.

Through the doorway of Stillness, the seemingly miraculous is revealed, old hurts surface to be released, and possibilities arise where there seemed to be none. Doors that were closed suddenly open, and the most mundane circumstance becomes a timeless moment to treasure. This is the exploration of a lifetime... simply listen to the words and music in The Power of Peace recording and let it take you *home* again...

THE PRACTICE

THE THREE BREATH AWARENESS
accessing the infinite peace that exists inside you... within moments

The Three Breath Awareness is the principal reconnection tool of The Simplicity of Stillness Method. It is a *gateway* for bringing the power of peace into your everyday life. Time slows down as you connect to a deeper sense of love, tranquility and well-being. You discover an ability to more readily access inspiration and the clarity required to make better decisions

Most people think they can't acquire or maintain this awareness because of their busy lives. With The Three Breath Awareness, that concept is broken. It isn't only about having time for lengthy meditations, it's about living in the *awareness* this state of peace offers you throughout the day – eyes open or closed.

To initiate or accelerate your connection, first listen to the Stillness Session CD accompanying this book. Once this connection has been established, you will be able to access it again so very easily.

It's not just about breathing. And it's not just about taking deep yogic-style breaths. It's about attuning to conscious awareness at all times; weaving it throughout your entire day. Once this life force Energy is integrated, you will be able to reconnect simply by returning to the breath with an inward focus – regardless of what is happening in your moment-to-moment reality.

When you use this process consistently, your connection to inspiration, strength, and wisdom expands exponentially. Once you access this power to align with your highest potential, you'll return to it again and again.

The Three Breath Awareness

This process can be done with your eyes open or closed. Practice initially with your eyes closed until you are able to reconnect within a few breaths.

- **Take a moment** to become present.
- **Close your eyes or find a point of focus**. You can be standing, sitting or laying down.
- **Begin breathing VERY DEEPLY.** Breathe so deep you feel the air moving throughout every cell in your body, from the top of your head to your toes.
- **Feel tension in your body releasing** with each breath.
- **Allow your focus to drift away** from the distractions of the outside world toward that deep serenity and awareness within. Feel everything slowing down…

- **After the third DEEP breath**, sit in the awareness of the Stillness within… (Your level of stress will determine the breaths needed to feel sensations of peace coming over you. In time you'll be able to access this shift in consciousness in only a breath. In the beginning it will likely take longer.)
- **Maintain this inner focus** for three to five minutes or longer.
- **With your eyes still closed, notice what has changed**, how you feel. Many people speak of a renewed feeling of calm in the body and often a tingling sensation in their hands or head as the Energy of peace circulates.
- **Open your eyes** and bring the Stillness and the awareness back with you into your day.

Using The Three Breath Awareness tool when going through difficulties of any kind will improve your state of mind in the moment as well as the outcomes you are looking for.

This Week's Practice:

Integrate this tool into your life now by closing your eyes and breathing into this very moment. Don't wait to practice The Three Breath Awareness when you are having a challenging day. Commit to doing this exercise at least once or twice a day, during a break at work, and again in the evening as a way to clear the slate. Within moments you'll discover how simple it is to access a deeper connection to the knowing within you.

stillness...
what does it mean to you...

tapping into your heart
breathing into the moment
feeling it guiding your actions
dancing with life, with your eyes wide open
all of the above

define it
so it can offer love
to anyone
who is ready to hear its call

profound, yes
practical, yes
all encompassing,
yes... yes... yes

CHAPTER 2

RELEASING RESISTANCE OR GOING BACK TO SLEEP

what is most natural to the human experience is to resist
change... and yet the rewards realized are worth every
ounce of self effort made

This voyage of discovery you have embarked on is designed
to reconnect you with your innate knowing, where you reclaim
your natural power, and open your life to a spectrum of
experiences that you might not have thought possible before
now. Our basic human tendencies are predisposed to going
back to *sleep* – while our higher selves search for those turning
points that literally force us into facing our fears and doing
whatever it takes to move into the next chapter of our personal
evolution.

The blueprint to facilitate this process contains cognizance
of our challenges, the beliefs we have accepted, personal and
collective – and an ability to stay open to the guidance we receive
in the many forms it arrives. In Eastern philosophy, Lord Ganesh
will *put* an obstacle in your path when he believes it to be the
best course of action to guide you to greater understanding and
freedom. Most people see them as *problems* but they are really
gifts in disguise that bring awareness to cultivate the internal
strength required for living a life of greater meaning.

When you resist anything, you constrict the conscious
Energy stream that accesses enlightened choices. Feeling angry,
overwhelmed or frustrated are all clues that you're resisting

something. When you connect with infinite intelligence whatever has blocked you is revealed; conscious choices alter your beliefs, habits and behavior, setting in motion the healing and outcomes you are truly searching for.

the clues are all around you and in you

You can *choose* to remain stuck in a static past, missing opportunities in the moment, or look deeper at what could be hidden that wants to be revealed. When you let go of resistance, you are able to respond in ways that are exceedingly beneficial to your overall well-being. Wanting life to be different without being willing to do anything about it is what has created the endless cycles of suffering humanity has lived in for eons.

When you feel emotions that are uncomfortable, the impulse is often to look away. In these moments we are far more likely to indulge our addictions, create drama in our relationships, or seek out distraction through other means. Although these diversions might help to pacify the moment, *looking away* often increases the chances that these feelings will be triggered and re-experienced again some time in the future.

Utilizing this occasion as an invitation to become aware of what blocks your connection to that loving stream of universal awareness creates opportunities to heal the emotional cause of the pain. We don't need to be professionals or specialists to know that blocked emotions have innumerable negative health results. Your body always tells you when you've been carrying too much emotional stress or negativity of any kind.

By inviting the life force Energy of peace into your life you can reconnect to that limitless dimension that is always open to the potential of the now. Over time you will find you are far less inclined to remain stuck in a static past and have become more flexible to recognizing the opportunities present in each moment, regardless of how challenging they might appear.

breaking free

What this chapter focuses on is your ability to break free, to leave behind paradigms of suffering, to wake up from the sleep of illusion and recognize your potential. You can *choose* new ways to deal with challenges once you are conscious of them. You can't change what you can't see.

In this chapter are stories of people caught up in cycles of frustration and pain, caused by unconscious resistant behavior, who used the practical methods offered here to restore their natural flowing energetic state. These tools and practices facilitate the release of any resistance you may be experiencing in your own life as well.

Once the connection has been established, simply being mindful of your breath utilizing The Three Breath Awareness, can be all that's needed to see an evolutionary way of BE-ing emerge... isn't now that perfect time?

WAY COOL ... SELENA'S NEW LIFE

Blue hairstreaks, towering high heels, and that 'shut upppp' lingo that says you're on your game. Selena was a funky, *cool* Latina stylist at a happening hair salon in Santa Monica, California. It wasn't the kind of place I would normally seek out, but I had taken a wrong turn with a hair color and was in need of finding help fast. When I discovered a salon right around the corner from my new home with talented staff, I was hooked.

It's dangerous territory to speak to people about their size, but I felt a need to broach the subject as a strong feeling of concern had come over me. By my third appointment, Selena looked *noticeably larger* than when we met: she had gained so much weight even her face had changed shape. The once petite lady whispered in response that she had recently become ill. When the pain in her back and legs had become unbearable Selena went to the hospital where they kept her for observation for a week. "I couldn't believe this was happening to me... the pain was excruciating." The diagnosis was *erythema nodosum* an inflammation of the skin that was so debilitating it became difficult for her to walk.

The doctors prescribed a host of medications, including steroids, and her body began to retain water as a result. Selena now had a weekly appointment at the hospital to check her blood and when needed she would join others with the same illness and hook up to machines that drained the excess fluid from their body. She was told there was no cure and would have to live with this disease her entire life. Selena had just turned 26.

I was six months into my new life, going through a divorce, learning how to speak about this energetic form of transcendence that had shifted my world, and finding that I wasn't very good at it. I invited Selena to attend a program, and her unvarnished response was, "I don't believe in anything like that." Her smile said it all, *Thanks... but nooo thanks*. Selena added, "I'll be just fine... really."

When I returned the next month Selena's body was even larger, and her life had become even more difficult. Standing on swollen legs with an aching back all day was taking its toll on her mentally and physically. This hard-working young woman was becoming seriously depressed; she was taking a lot of medication, and the weekly hospital visits consistently reminded her of the fun life she no longer lived. I asked her again, with a *what have you got to lose, something might happen to give you new insight, and, at the very least, you would only be bored for a couple of hours* invitation. This time, she said yes. I'm not sure why, maybe she thought she'd lose a client if she didn't, as I know my ability to communicate what transpired in programs had definitely not improved.

* * *

"Okay. Not bad," was Selena's response to the program when I inquired a few days later. "Have you noticed anything different?" I wanted her to spend a moment in reflection, as the subtleties of this awakening Energy can happen for some so quietly, that you could miss it if you're not looking. A smile came across her face. "Come to think of it, something did happen. It usually takes me about 45 minutes to get to work and I get *road rage* at all the crazies out there – but the very next day when I got in my car, I suddenly found a talk radio program that was so funny I laughed all the way to work! The doctors think my sickness is stress related, so laughing is good for me. Yeah, that was pretty cool."

Synchronicity?? Hmmm. However you want to look at it life began to shift for Selena. Imagine the difference if you spent hours a day in your car screaming at people, or if you could flow with whatever comes your way and enjoy the time. Selena was more relaxed than I'd seen her in months. "Now I laugh all the way to work. Isn't that great?!"

Awareness began to permeate every area of Selena's life. Within a few months she left the salon where she worked and found a new place of employment. "Why are you changing jobs?" I had grown accustomed to the trendy salon, and enjoyed watching the many colorful stories of life walk in and out of that 3rd Street Promenade parade.

"I don't know. It just doesn't feel good to be here anymore." Selena was having difficulty clarifying what was guiding her, but you could see that she had a *knowing* that the move would be in her best interest. Her resistance to new ideas had diminished to such an extent, she embraced whatever showed up in her life – even big changes she didn't see coming.

A couple of months later, Selena and her boyfriend got an eviction notice – their apartment building had been sold: they had to move. Selena wasn't even upset. She felt everything was meant to be, took it in her stride and began searching for a new place. "I found one that's even better than where I was! I really like it!! There's more light, it's a *happier* place." It seemed as though the Universe was conspiring to give Selena a better life. Anything that didn't support her in finding balance – just began to shut down.

A workout studio opened nearby and she could get there easily in the middle of a workday. Selena liked it so much she joined an exercise boot camp. Her body got stronger. The weight began to drop off. She wouldn't have three drinks at the bar with friends, but one or two, and would leave earlier to make sure she could get up for her workouts. Nutritious foods became appealing and fried foods began disappearing as her body naturally craved food that matched her new lifestyle.

* * *

Each time I came for my hair appointment that field of infinite Energy would heighten as we shared special time together. We talked about love and money and boyfriends and different ways to deal with the practical aspects of life. The cynical young woman I had met became a powerhouse of strength who shared the light she was with everyone in her life. Her illness journey contributed to her immense compassion for anyone facing health issues. The *wild child* became a mainstay of support for her family and friends in ways that were unexplainable even to her. Selena was the one they now turned to for love and guidance. When her 11-year-old niece contracted leukemia, Selena was by her side, loving her, assisting her with whatever she needed, including insight for dealing with her own death.

* * *

The gifts flowing into Selena's life were gradual and nonstop. She became stronger day by day, month by month. This pint-sized powerhouse became so in tune with her body that she knew instinctively when she was pushing too hard, and would immediately slow down, breathe deep and connect with that infinite intelligence that was sending her messages of enlightened guidance. Selena began to question why she needed the same amount of medication she'd been given when originally diagnosed. One day she told her doctors she would like to begin paring down her daily doses. They didn't agree with her decision – insisting that *she had to face facts – she had a life-long illness and nothing would change that.*

The choices Selena made in the months ahead were made by a woman who wanted to participate in her well-being. She wanted to work *with* the doctors, *and* she didn't want to take prescription drugs if they weren't needed. Each month she took fewer pills and observed if her body would stay balanced. When she reached the six-month celebration of being healthy without taking *any* drugs, she went for testing.

It was at this time the doctors told her that they might have *misdiagnosed her illness, as they couldn't find a trace of the disease in her body.* How often do people who have unexplained remission hear this today? When reality doesn't match conventional knowledge, often the explanation given – *it never existed* – is easier than spending time researching what could actually initiate this level of natural healing in someone's life. In *Spontaneous Evolution* renowned scientist, Bruce Lipton, comments on how healings can occur when an individual consciously or even unconsciously makes a significant change in their beliefs and behaviors.[1] The good news is we each get to decide what we believe, the choice is ours alone to make.

…one year later

Passing the hospital room where Selena had gone for the weekly treatments that drained her of life's joy, she saw some of the same people still sitting there. Selena got how blessed she was to have released the resistance she had to discovering tools that would support her throughout her life. While she admits that she doesn't totally *get* how this life force intelligence could transform her life in the way it did, it doesn't matter to her anymore.

Today, Selena's still *way cool*, occasionally with rainbow hair and always with those super-high heels – only now she's figured out how to live in a way that's not life threatening – it's life enhancing. How very cool is that…

If synchronicity is not appearing in your life, you might not be in the flow that creates it.

Anytime you are anxious, frustrated or overwhelmed – Become Present – in that moment:
- Do The Three Breath Awareness
- Reconnect to that Energy stream of pure inspiration…

- Write in your Journal what habits you have become aware of that don't support your being in the flow of life. Your awareness of these patterns supports new choices, transforming your behaviors from the core, where unconscious beliefs exist.

WORDLESS INSIGHTS
the blue yonder of possibility

A shock of white hair made him stand out even more than his 6'4" height and commanding build. The image of the Marlboro man riding across a Western frontier came to mind, only it was Amsterdam, 2006. Evidently a friend had insisted he come; yet there wasn't any resistance in his posture, rather a sense of total absorption as he quietly immersed himself in every element of information given.

It was a stormy winter day; rain cascaded down beyond the curtained windows of the cozy room where the retreat was held. In every full-day program, there are times spent in Stillness, where the aware presence in the space offers people whatever they are ready to open to in their lives. Much like riding a horse heading out into *the blue yonder* – anything is possible.

This could be the day for a wild ride on a bucking horse that can't be tamed, similar to the mind, or it could be the day for a gentle walk, similar to the nurturing embrace of a loved one. Then again, you could find yourself on a runaway ride that takes you into mysterious surroundings where you are so moved by what you see and feel, you want every second to last a lifetime. You never know what will transpire, until it does.

As the retreat came to a close, the Marlboro man whose name was Patrick spoke for the first time. It was in measured tones, as though he had to search for the words he voiced. "I have the impression that what has happened is that I've been reconnected to something I was connected to when I came into this world." Everyone *felt* what he was trying to convey. It was like a force field, a sound wave that grew in strength as it rippled out from him into the space. There was a hush in the room as he concluded his thoughts, "… and from now on… the strength of that connection will grow… It gives wordless insights… I'm very happy." He smiled briefly and went back into the Stillness from where his words had arisen.

* * *

A year had passed before I saw Patrick again: this time the Marlboro man showed up in Vienna, Austria. The crevices that had lined his face, revealing the stress of a hard-lived existence, had disappeared and were replaced by the look of a person who is okay with life, and inspired by its passage. Patrick spoke of the many changes that had transpired. He had been through a lot of rough terrain and the end result was that he stopped drinking. After *30 years* of consuming a quart of whiskey a day, he stopped drinking. Life was changing, there seemed to be no turning back.

It had been seven months since he made that decision. Along the way, Patrick began having more of the *wordless insights* he had spoken of before, and was ready now to look even deeper. At the end of the evening's program, he left rather quickly. I didn't know where Patrick had gone on the next step in his evolutionary journey until a few days later when he could relate what had happened on that night.

During the Stillness Session Patrick began having visions that didn't feel like dreams, but more like reality; "I was floating face down in a river. My body was completely white, leading me to believe I had been dead for quite some time. Suddenly I felt someone grab my right arm. As I looked up to see who was lifting me... I saw Jesus..." Patrick shared his vision as someone would who had just seen something completely out the spectrum of his life experience. In an incredulous voice, and yet with complete conviction, he continued, "I want you to understand that I've never been religious. I don't go to church or practice any form of structured religion. This is a total surprise to me. It *was Jesus*. I saw him *clearly*.

"And then... someone began to pull on my left arm, I looked up and..." Patrick's wife, who was standing beside him, interjected, "Was it me?" "No dear," he said gently, "it was *Mary*."

The experience affected Patrick so intensely, the following evening he attended Saint Stephan's Cathedral, where as *chance* would have it, there was a special performance of *Ave Maria*. The *intangible* was showing up quite tangibly in Patrick's life. His health, his state of mind, his judgments, likes and dislikes, were all dissolving into a place of acceptance. Love was the loudest note being played and even though his mind could have railed against these experiences as delusional or impossible, Patrick listened to what his heart presented him.

as this stream of boundless life energy dissolves our concepts...
what appears is divine love, even if we are not aware
of what that is

That same year, during an evening program in Santa Monica, California, the room filled with that tangible Energy of sweetness, like swimming in a sea of honeyed calm. A woman of Latin descent spoke of the Virgin Mary with a sense of intoxication, "I saw her... she was standing right here. She was here with all of us." From the far side of the room a man shared that Jesus had appeared to him. Another person spoke of an Indian master of meditation, whose presence was felt by more than a few; while another spoke of Buddha, radiantly offering blessings. Everyone felt the sacredness of this special night.

The wordless insights we are all given, those that help a man stop drinking after 30 years, and those that allow people to experience the many forms of their own personal truth are the gifts being given to all of us in this unique time we are living in. Regardless of what resistance or addiction has taken you on a ride, as this field of conscious awareness expands, the experience of Love arrives in many forms. Remaining *asleep* is no longer an option. You can find what you need to heal any pain that has ever locked you in its overpowering grip.

The breeze at dawn has secrets to tell you...
Don't go back to sleep
You must ask for what you really want
Don't go back to sleep
People are going back and forth across the doorsill
where the two worlds touch
The door is round and open
Don't go back to sleep.
~ Rumi

Everyone becomes illumined by the force of pure Love, and when it reverberates through you, as it did for Patrick, and for so many on that night in Santa Monica, there is really nothing left to say. Wordless insights... the power of Love, the power of knowing who you truly are...

THE ANGRY MAN

The early morning rays streamed soft light on the ebullient group that gathered for breakfast. Everyone was dressed in their finest temple clothes. A kaleidoscope of colors and patterns, floral and checks blended, creating a sense of harmony among the group as a whole. It was a several-hour drive to get to the base of the volcano and there was a feeling of anticipation as the van took off. It was an auspicious day – something special was brewing. Just what that was, we would soon find out.

Watching life stream by my window, the screen filled with mopeds, families with babies heading down the two-lane highway and an assortment of unique characters moving in a cultural dance. On one side of the road were soccer players and kids in uniforms – if you didn't see the temples in the distance, you could think you were in mainstream USA. On the other side, old women with beautiful sun-carved faces stooped under the weight of the firewood they carried. And always – the smiling faces.

The road down into the volcano twists and turns. The landscape is breathtaking: vibrant greens amidst rivers of black lava rock left from the fires that burned everything in the last eruption. Ahead is the lake. It seems quiet today. Another gift; maybe we will have the temple to ourselves. Mount Batur is one of the most sacred temples in all of Bali. According to Kadek, our Balinese friend, it is on the same grid lines that run through Machu Picchu in Peru.

* * *

In the parking entrance to the grounds we are met by a local villager, his wife, and son. They will be joining us for the ceremony. I ask Kadek to translate. As I speak I notice that a few men have begun to gather around our group. One man in particular seems very angry. He is pacing, walking in circles, looking at me intensely. He tries to pull the photographer who is documenting this day away from the group. Later she described how distressing it felt to be near the overpowering antagonistic energy he was emitting. She worried that his seething anger could become volatile.

I see this angry man out of the corner of my eye and wonder why he is so enraged. But I know my purpose is to take care of those who are drawing this grace into their lives, and so I keep my focus. I decide to share the following story I had once heard on a Deepak Chopra tape, as it symbolizes humanity's unconscious nature and the strange situation we have found ourselves in.

A scientific test was done where fish were placed in a tank. A glass partition divided their living quarters in half. One day, the scientists removed the wall, doubling the space the fish could live in. *The fish never swam to the other side.* They continued to live within borders that no longer imprisoned them. It was reported that the fish couldn't go to the other side because of their limited view of the world. *They could only see what they first knew to be the perimeters of their universe.*[1]

Is it the same for all of us? What can't we see? Could there be more for us to know, just beyond that wall?

* * *

Spiders line the entrance of the lava-rock sculptured gates, the sun envelops us in its warmth, and blue skies become the dome crowning this jewel of days. We sit at the foot of the most sacred shrine where the axis is believed to be that protects the island of Bali. Vibrant notes from the Stillness Session music echo through the temple and resound with the peace that guides everyone into the depths of indefinable silence.

, This dynamic Energy pulsates through my hands and after spending a moment with each person I suddenly notice, at the back of the group... the angry man. *Why has he come? What am I to do?* He beckons to me. I am hesitant. I wonder if he will lash out. Then I am guided to trust. As I touch the top of his head, that universal principle expresses an Energy of intensity that causes him to sway, heralding the wonderment of what is about to unfold. The music plays on. When everyone's eyes open, the angry man can't stop shouting. The villager rushes to his side managing to translate his words almost as rapidly as they are being spoken. "What was that?? It felt amazing!! Why didn't you tell us what this was before??!!" The questions don't stop, and neither does his joyous enthusiasm. "We will have the whole village come!!"

* * *

How is it possible that someone that indignant and outraged, after only a few moments of experiencing absolute peace, becomes this joyful, light-hearted, loving human being? We were speechless. This individual's pain, once released, filled him with love for those he had condemned, and now he implored me to offer him the blessed waters of the temple. As he drank, I felt that we were both drinking in waters of awareness. Was this angry man a messenger so I could understand more fully what I hadn't yet grasped?

Anger, hostility and resistance are lowly adversaries in the face of pure Love. This man's hatred and animosity were dissolved with such potency all that was left was the essence of Love inherent in his own heart, which was now streaming out from him to all of us. *The fish swam to the other side of the tank… and the world became a beautiful place.*

When resistance dissolves, what separates us from knowing we are all forms of love can open *in a moment*; a blessed gap in the bias that reinforces our conceptual boundaries. When the arc of a man's rage diminishes, the heavens rain peace and hope down like cleansing showers soothing this earth.

epilogue

When I began traveling the world after I heard the message that I was to offer this stream of infinite Energy to humanity, I couldn't have imagined all that I would be shown. The journey and the people I met along the way taught me what is possible as this field of intelligence is accessed. I feel certain this was one of those days that all of us present will never forget.

Why was the man so angry? Where did he come from? Why did he ask to experience what I was offering when he was so undeniably angered and in conflict with it or with me?

I know that I am the delivery person; I show up to bring people the package their soul is asking for. I don't believe I have to *understand* everything; what I see with my own eyes and what I experience tells me all I need to know. How could someone in that state of agitation move into a state of joyfulness within only moments after this divine Energy ignited within him? I don't know that I will ever have the perfect answer. I was astounded. We all were. And yet, we were there to be witness to what is possible. Knowing this inspired me to believe that there is even more we haven't begun to comprehend. And, the gates are opening...

As I laid my head down on my pillow that evening, my thoughts were of gratitude and prayer – to always keep waking up... and waking up... and waking up again.

INVITE IN THAT ENERGY FLOW

There is a flow of life... when you tap into it... it reminds you when to become still.

All you need to do... is close your eyes and allow that honeyed calm to move through the cells in your body...

Within moments... you've released whatever constricted you and feel inspired to begin again... Invite that tranquil Energy to flow into your life... now

THE PRACTICE

RELEASING RESISTANCE... HEALING THE PAIN

recognizing when something wants to change...
is an opening to a world of possibility

Resistance is a natural inhibitor that disconnects you from the infinite Energy stream of life. When you are in pain, feeling angry, overwhelmed, frustrated, or even lethargic, and can recognize it's a signal that something in your life wants to change – it can be of great benefit. Where it becomes problematic is when it inflames your mind and negative patterns begin playing old tapes. Taking any action from a state of pessimism, indignation, or irritation is never a good idea.

Resistance is often associated with an intense emotional sensation pumping through your system. You feel out of control, unconscious tendencies beg to reclaim your addictions – similar to what was experienced by many of the people written about in this chapter, 'Releasing Resistance... or Going Back to Sleep'. From life-threatening health risks to complete physical exhaustion, all reminders of the vital importance to continually release the *stuck* energy of fear, worry, and pretense from your body.

Intellectualizing what *isn't working* – won't help. Neither will blaming life or others. It's actually quite difficult to go into Stillness when you are in this state of mind. Once you let go of the pent-up emotion, you become more resourceful; self-imposed limitations, blocks, and boundaries that have shaped your life disappear, and a world of possibility opens.

The Practice of Releasing Resistance
Part 1

- **Physical movement.** Do something physical to get this *blocked emotion* out of your body – work out in a gym, take a power yoga class, ride a bike, or take a walk in the park.
- **Watch a funny movie** and laugh till you cry.
- **Vocal expression.** Yell into a pillow or sing out loud to expel any blocked emotions.
- **Get in water**, in a pool, tub or shower, and release worry and

tension by allowing the soothing waters to wash them away. Imagine standing under a waterfall where each drop cleanses your mind as well as your body.

Do any of one of these methods or a combination of them. It seems too simple and yet it works every time. As negative thoughts diminish, it becomes easier to renew your connection to the peace and creativity at your core. Once these blocks of painful emotion are diffused, connecting back to the healing stream of pure peace can be as simple as breathing deep.

Part 2

- **Use The Three Breath Awareness** – Notice how quickly your resourcefulness returns.
- **Listen to a Stillness Session –** If emotions come up, be with them, feel the Love in your heart melting everything in its path.

As your awareness grows, over time you'll find that you respond differently to life's challenges. When your beliefs change, so do your habits; you are more in alignment with your vision of who you see yourself to be. Much of the anger and pain you might have lived with has been subtly transformed. You aren't as affected by what used to make you anxious, worried, or upset. It's an ongoing journey. Just turn down the new road, and stop going down the one you're on. Consider new points of view. Consider taking on even more beliefs that will empower you.

This Week's Practice:

- **Reflect** on where you are experiencing resistance or the emotional symptoms of it in your life.

- **Write in your journal** what you want to let go of, and what you want to attain.
- **Release: Choose any of the methods above.** Experiment with the different processes until you feel the resistance dissolving.
- **Listen to the Stillness Session CD.** Allow the peace to dissolve any angst and remind you of the Love at your core.
- **Write down any new insights.** Reflect and take action on the inspiration given.

When resistance is replaced with the free-flowing energy of possibility, life becomes the game you want to play. The many adventures that await you could be similar to what Selena, Patrick, and The Angry Man discovered – to just be open, flexible and ready... for whatever comes your way... then release and let go... and smile...

CHAPTER 3

RECLAIMING YOUR INNATE POWER... CONNECTING WITH YOUR INNER TEACHER

we have entered an important stage in the evolution of humanity where we stop looking for answers outside ourselves and turn our focus inward toward the infinite intelligence of all that is...

As the saying goes... *When the student is ready, the teacher appears.* An integral way of reclaiming your innate power is by attuning to the wisdom of the heart, accessing the eloquent Energy of life, and connecting with your inner teacher. This process involves turning the volume down on the many distractions of the outside world and amplifying the *voice* that speaks to you from within. As I mentioned in the last chapter, the blueprint to facilitate this process includes being open to your soul's influence and listening to the inherent brilliance... of your *own inner teacher.*

One of the best ways to hear that *voice* or those *insights* is by consciously inviting moments of Stillness into your life. As you read in the chapter on 'Releasing Resistance or Going Back to Sleep', this time of discovery requires an increased willingness to look closely at whatever challenges you – not to resolve all your problems at once – but rather to plant the seeds of what you would like to see change. What new traits do you want to develop? What new habits will sustain the positive qualities you wish to incorporate into your life?

a new stream of guidance

It's fascinating to observe what occurs when you place direct attention on anything from this universal dimension of consciousness; a new stream of guidance begins to filter through. It even educates you to ask better questions so you can find more meaningful answers.

The information you receive is revealed in a variety of forms. It isn't when you've said, 'I had a gut feeling', and it is also not an *aha* moment. It resonates even deeper. It's an insight, not an impulse. It could come from a chance conversation, a synchronistic connection, a book falling off a shelf, a moment in Stillness. The information deepens your understanding of the boundless nature of life and your connection to it. In time you will begin to trust that whenever you have a pressing question or concern, the answer of what to do is always there. Just notice when anything strikes a new note within you. The clarity that emerges will be like a river washing clean your window to the world.

As the light of consciousness expands your capacity to listen from a depth of understanding you might not have known before, it initiates your inner teacher to speak with greater coherence. This wise counsel can present itself in myriad forms, from a gentle reminder – to an explosion of newfound enthusiasm, passion, and excitement. In this chapter you will discover how the trajectories of life's events that guide you to extraordinary life circumstances occur through the transformative influence of your inner teacher.

If you are a longtime meditator or have been practicing Stillness for a while, the Stillness Session audio can simply be added to your existing practices. The conscious Energy transmitted through these recordings offers you whatever will expand your field of awareness. We are all teachers *and* students, and similar to the people you will read about in this chapter, when we connect with the gift we are, there is so much more available to share with the world around us.

the fire of truth

As the alchemy of Truth reawakens your natural state of being, it burns away what feels like lifetimes of confusion. The journey then is to sustain and magnify this healing vibration. The SOS Practice at the end of this chapter is designed to help you deepen your understanding of the untapped wisdom and potential that you already have. Everything you need is inside you. All that's left to do now is to open and allow space in your life for this expansive awareness to grow.

THE DROPPED CALL

They were simple letters, forming words on a page that today carried meaning in a way they never had before. Similar to bubbles that rise to the top as water is about to boil – this loyal, hard-working employee stood up from her chair, walked into her boss's office and told him exactly how she felt. In that moment, Sandy allowed the steam that had been contained for 17 years to be released. How many people had been damaged by her boss's *words*; disturbing, demeaning, demoralizing words that wreaked havoc in many people's lives every time they were unleashed. It had to end – at least for her – and today was the day.

Sandy packed her things and walked out the door. "I knew that I would never let anyone speak to me in that way again! I don't know why I let it go on for so long." The woman who walked out of that office on the dusty back roads of Laughlin, Nevada was not the same woman who had walked in just a few hours earlier. She felt clarity in her heart and mind, giving her the inspiration to take action in the many areas of her life that had been in *park* instead of *drive*. And so she did just that – drove straight to a real estate office and signed the necessary papers to put their home on the market. It was time for a change, and the road to this new adventure was now wide open. Sandy was thrilled with the freedom she felt as she left behind all that had imprisoned her for so many years.

There's a false sense of security in believing that if we keep everything as it is, even if it's uncomfortable, we will be *safe*. It's an illusion. Nothing could be farther from the truth. *If I just keep my head down and keep the status quo, nothing will ever hurt me*. It's the pinnacle of delusion. And so our deepest cries become smothered by our fears, and we get locked into living a life of hidden anguish, instead of the meaningful, joyous adventure that our life can be. Sandy was discovering a new kind of freedom, and from more than one prison on that fateful day.

* * *

John and Sandy were rock-solid folks, loyal, caring, and uncomplicated. They had shown up in my life exactly when I needed friends to support me; sitting on their sofa, watching football so I didn't have to think was a simple form of rehabilitation as years of drug addiction were released. We'd lost touch over the years, and destiny had recently placed us back in each other's lives.

One of the ways you begin to comprehend the incomprehensible is when you experience it or see the effects of it in your life. The series of unfolding events we all became witness to demonstrated very clearly how this field of intelligence reaches beyond our self-defined limitations of distance and time. Twenty-four hours before that fateful day when she took her life back, Sandy was on an SOS teleseminar-type call, wanting to experience whatever this *expansion of consciousness* was that had changed my life. She was only briefly on the call when her line disconnected. After several attempts to rejoin the program Sandy became resigned, believing she was just not going to *get it* on that day. Later that afternoon we spoke and I assured her that she had *gotten* whatever would bring her closer to knowing her true essence.

This magnified field of consciousness invites everyone present, regardless of where they are geographically, to enter into a space of universal Stillness. This is the electromagnetic field that pervades all space and the cosmos, whether we fully comprehend it or not.

Within hours after that *dropped call* Sandy's heightened perception allowed her to see what she couldn't before, and she now had the courage to face what she couldn't *do* before that very moment. She expressed herself easily once the cloak of her unconsciousness came off. It was time to make some changes; to move from a job where she wasn't valued, to move geographically from where she and John had been living, and to stop accepting that age-old idiom, *it's-just-the-way-it-is* and realize she had the ability to shift any part of her life that wasn't working.

A chapter was ending and even though this very stable homemaker didn't know what would be next, she wanted to keep moving forward; she trusted her *knowing* that selling their home would prepare them for whatever came next. When I later asked Sandy's husband of 26 years how he felt when his wife, seemingly out of the blue, put their home on the market – he responded with a wink, the signal of a husband who's decided how much simpler life can be when you go with the flow. "I knew whatever Sandy did would turn out just fine."

* * *

I wasn't aware of any of these unusual incidents when I invited the two of them to join me in Lake Tahoe at a wedding I was attending so we could catch up on all that was new in our lives. It would be the first time after an 18-year gap that we'd be together. Years seemed to have passed in a day, which is how it is when you're connected through the heart. But my longtime friend did take me by surprise when she mentioned in a very matter-of-fact manner, "Oh, by the way... I never told you what happened after that call. My whole life changed."

As the wind whispered through the giant fir trees surrounding our rustic cabin in the woods, I learned for the first time about the many unexpected events that had transpired. Sandy was listening to her inner knowing. As she did, more and more messages arrived to show her, not *how* things would work out, but that with trust they always would. She was in the driver's seat, creating from the inspiration that was guiding her toward an exciting new future.

Sandy's expanded awareness seemed to have a profound effect on her husband's life as well. John received a call from a former employee whose new company had become so successful he wanted to meet and discuss some creative opportunities. And, as it turned out, my flight to Tahoe actually landed in the city, where the interview was to take place! The domino effect was fully underway.

* * *

John's first foray into the presence of his timeless nature occurred when we stopped for a Stillness break in the vibrant forests surrounding Lake Tahoe. He had never done any form of meditation and hadn't really been interested, but what I explained made sense to him through his study of science and quantum physics.

John and Sandy spent their lives like so many good-hearted folks, raising a family and helping others whenever they could. They had their share of good times as well as struggles, but something had shifted, they'd become a magnet for good news, and it just kept coming.

anything is possible… when you believe it is

John had tumors on his face that doctors told him were impossible to remove, so he should *just get used to having them.* Unfortunately, one was located right in the middle of his face where you couldn't ignore it. I didn't know how, but I believed they would be gone soon, and felt he should begin looking for answers. When the newly inspired couple returned home, John met with a doctor who told him it wouldn't be easy, *but it was possible.* After he removed the tumors, another gift appeared – he wouldn't accept any money for the surgery. The doctor knew of John's charitable work and just wanted to thank him in the best way he could.

The synchronicity didn't stop; even before John and Sandy returned home, John was offered that position in Reno to become president of the company, doubling the salary he now had! And they wanted him to begin within 30 days! Since John and Sandy had recently sold their home, it was easy to say yes. Anytime they wanted guidance on what their next step would be, all they had to do was *Make a Request*[1] to the universal field of intelligence that had already delivered numerous gifts. They weren't even surprised when they found a new home in an area they were told they couldn't afford. The insights they received were to look where they wanted to live. They listened. The result: the house was *waiting* for them, *and*, with the right price tag.

A whole new life and peace of mind… What John and Sandy did that was uncommon was to take action on their inspiration, and the power of the magnetic field of their thoughts and intentions rapidly demonstrated how they could participate in the creation of their lives. While this amount of change might have been challenging, Sandy said it gave them a new lease on life. Their marriage became stronger, and they made plans together for entering this time of empowered adventure in their lives. They remembered how to breathe through the challenges when they would arise, and trusted that new insight would always appear.

It's really amazing what all can happen from a *dropped call*… especially one where destiny is on the other end of the line.

Without the clarity that we can participate in our future, it's easy to become resigned and believe the power to change anything exists outside us, instead of within us.

It isn't only about knowing the laws of attraction…
Connecting to higher intelligence is key…

- Listen to the Stillness Session Recording.
- Write the messages received and take action on the inspiration.

CEO
From Depression to Elation

Plenty of money, beautiful wife, three healthy daughters, good friends, and all the trappings success can give you. It should have been the best of times, and yet Nils was hurting. He couldn't remember any particular incident leading to the depression that derailed his world like a runaway train between an ever-widening chasm, plunging into that frightening void of no return. One day, without any advance warning, all the happiness he had ever known seemed to be drained from his life. The struggle continued for over two years, the pain intensifying until, "It exploded, in a feeling of being lived by the fires of each day with no energy to enjoy my family or other gifts around me."

His family and friends in Amsterdam, and from around the world, had suggestions to help Nils get back on track, from various medical and alternative treatments to psychiatry and counseling, which in his words, all led him: "... to a seriously negative state of being unable to cope with small events, or even spend time with the ones dearest to me, which intensified my frustration and negative feelings even more. I did not know what to do or where to turn to improve this situation, not only for me but more for my family. I felt I was letting them down terribly."

One day when Nils was researching a treatment suggested by a relative, he *somehow* landed on my website. How this could have happened was quite unforeseeable, as there were no links or references to what he was looking for on my site, and yet, when it's time to reclaim that inherent power, intriguing coincidences show up everywhere. The words in the letter Nils wrote were not in his native tongue, but each page clarified the feelings of awakening that are stirring inside so many people today. "I felt an immediate excitement. I needed to get in touch with this experience you were telling about. I could not explain exactly what the story [on your website] was telling. I could not even conceive a glimpse; however I would give an arm to get near to this exciting experience."

He would have done anything, or gone wherever he needed to go to find what had begun to resonate within him. Once again, the universe orchestrated an unexpected surprise. He wouldn't have to travel anywhere; I was giving programs in Amsterdam, *one week* from the day he was led to find what that longing in his heart was truly all about!

It is this thirst that has caused humankind to search for meaning throughout the centuries. It's for the Love that never dies, even when our bodies leave this earth, it's what exists throughout all time. You can't know this joy when you're in pain, I know, I tried. Maybe you can taste the righteous anguish that often writers believe is needed so that their pain is *noble*, but this sensation is fleeting and doesn't touch the panoramic colors of ecstatic expression that you *experience* once that field of loving intelligence opens.

* * *

Nils was finding his own way. His depression had become a driving force of great significance in his life. More synchronicities began to occur, those that bring the simplest pleasures. This solicitor of diligent performance was running quite late, as traffic on the crowded freeways to Utrecht rival those of all major cities, when suddenly he spotted the next answer to his quest. There in front of the building, just waiting for him, was – a parking spot! He walked into the program just as the lights went down... arriving... right on time.

When an invitation to go into meditation is made, our friend, the mind, can often choose this time for futile chatter: good news, bad news, old and new news, likes, dislikes, opinions and judgments. Whatever is going on usually speaks very loudly until it comes into the presence of a stronger vibration. The Energy of absolute peace resonated within the physical space through the words and music; Nils felt the movement through his body as he closed his eyes. When it's time for us to awaken to higher consciousness, there's nothing that can stop it from happening, no matter where we are or what surrounds us. For Nils, it arrived in waves:

"... an extremely pleasant and peaceful feeling... and extreme heat, showed me a first glimpse of what I was about to get into much deeper. I wanted to maintain this experience... then a cloud of emotion started pouring over me, a warm feeling like a golden tingling shower, relieving what had been there... letting go deeper after each breath.

"It led to an immense peaceful brightness, warmth, and joy. It filled me with such peace and relaxation I did not want to leave. I was so impressed by this experience I could hardly speak."

Nils's depression and struggles began to disappear as the light of Truth illuminated the dark corners where his pain had been hiding. The winter winds swept cold air across the Netherlands, but the heat Nils generated from the Love he was experiencing warmed the hearts of all he encountered. Life would never be the same.

This is the true mystery of our existence, the one worth searching for, longing for, praying for. It isn't that Nils would never have a difficult day again, but the journey had begun. This is the odyssey he'll share with his children and grandchildren, not from a mountaintop, but from the daily joy of being in life, running a business, honoring his employees, and loving his wife and family. Nils's elation came from being connected to that profoundly illuminating, deeply tranquil state of absolute peace.

* * *

I saw Nils one year later in Vienna when he arrived to discover what mysteries could be now revealed that would take him even deeper. He said there had been times of doubt during the last months, which led him to making Stillness Sessions and The Practices a higher priority. He recognized that connection to his own strength grew in direct proportion to integrating these new habits into his life. He also spoke about the pain and depression that originally drew him to find this healing awareness, and that it hadn't shown up again.

Our struggles can be viewed as a gift when we recognize that they can guide us to the greatest knowledge life has to offer – not one any amount of success can buy – but the one that brings enlightened wisdom from within.

epilogue

Nils's experiences healed his suffering and empowered him with a state of mental health and well-being that brought balance to his life. When any mists of confusion or doubt arrived in the coming year, his inner teacher consistently reminded him who he was beyond the illusion his mind wanted to create.

Nils is a happy man today living with the ups and downs we all face, only they don't register in the way they used to, and he has created a new career that aligns more with his interests in health. How very interesting, that our greatest difficulties often lead us to what we are here to share with others, and these challenges can also bring us into direct connection with the most insightful teacher of all – the undeniable wisdom of your innate brilliance.

LISTEN, LISTEN, LISTEN...

As you open to the answers that come from being in connection to this indefinable power – the 'wins' achieved are those that align with your very soul.

In this way, you 'win' instantly whether you see the results immediately or not.

The person you've become wins battles of great import purely by the strength of your loving conviction to honor yourself and all of humankind.

Realize that you are divinely guided...
And... Listen, Listen, Listen...

LISTENING TO THE MESSAGES
wisdom can be heard from that field of infinite
intelligence when we listen... just listen...

A new sphere of awareness opens as you connect to the stream of life's infinite Energy; it's like entering an information highway with search engine optimization already programmed to find wisdom and enlightened guidance at every stop. You are directed from a higher understanding, rather than feeling like you are consistently downloading thoughts and images of senseless knowledge that often resulted in overload. In this chapter people connected to that limitless dimension and followed the signals they received, each in their own way, to access solutions to living and creating their life in alignment with their highest values and aspirations.

Many people feel frustrated that they don't have answers to the important questions in their lives, that they just don't get messages in any form. Is it possible the messages were always there only we didn't have the capacity to see them or hear the broadcast? Just as science tell us that elephants have a way of communicating that resonates on sound levels humans can't hear – could it be possible that we are also unable to see and hear what has been beyond our (vibrational) comprehension, and what our unconscious beliefs defined as real? Maybe we just can't see or hear clearly until we access *the conscious* awareness that releases these outdated belief boundaries.

In a recent report from *60 Minutes*, a small group of people stepped forward to demonstrate that our brains are capable of much more than we have ever dreamed; these people have the capacity to recall everything that happened on any given day in their lives, and in history, within seconds of asking them. Everything! From what they had for breakfast to what the headlines were in the newspaper. They are not savants; they just have a skill that very few of us have. If this is possible, then what else is there that we haven't yet considered?

Once your awareness expands, you are able to break through the societal concepts that have hindered our evolution, and begin exploring your innate genius.[1] Similar to John and Sandy, and Nils, you will discover ways of *listening* that invite and bring this new form of communication into your daily life. The signs will be everywhere.

If you wait to hear a booming voice or see an illuminating vision – you could wait a long time. Then again, anything is possible, and this kind of experience has happened to many people. If you want to develop a course of action that directs your life from a place of purpose and love, learn to listen to the messages that are being sent your way. This is not about becoming psychic, or telepathic, it's about attuning to your inner teacher. Will you have the perfect answer to everything? You will, but that means trusting the journey, what works and what doesn't and what you are meant to learn from *both* circumstances. You are here to discover and allow the unfolding of your life's journey in the best way possible – and it will… moment-by-moment and day-by-day.

Messages come in many forms – often those that seem too simplistic are the ones that make the mundane of life so much fun. As you observe and confirm for yourself the synchronicities that now appear regularly, you will really enjoy the exquisite game that life has become.

The messages can appear in various forms:

- A deep knowing from within.
- When listening to a friend or a child, or someone speaking on TV or other media, and unexpectedly, a bell rings inside you.
- An illness or injury that suddenly stops you in your tracks and forces you to look at your life in a whole new light.
- Not getting what you thought you wanted – which is an invitation to recognize that even what you can't see clearly now, could be guiding you to a better outcome than the one you thought was best – literally forcing you to look deeper.
- Signs on billboards. (Really!! Yes, happens all the time.) Also, newspaper articles that catch your eye, a letter or an email arrives with information that seems to be specifically answering the question you were holding in your mind.

The Practice of Listening to the Messages:

The Simplicity of Stillness Practices that assist you in tuning in to informed insights are:

- **Contemplation & Journaling** – Reflection brings forth new insights. Writing solidifies them. Clarity is revealed through your connection with the field of infinite intelligence where solutions await your inquiry and contemplation.
- **Stillness Sessions** – Time spent in the purified Energy of peace opens a gateway of wisdom where signals arrive.
- **Making Requests** – Much like a focused beam of light – *requests* invite messages to be revealed through many forms.

This Week's Practice:

- **Choose one concern or question** where you would like to receive a message.

- **Write it in your journal,** leaving space to write the answers that appear in the week ahead.
- **Choose one of The Practices** from above – and follow the guidelines.
- **Document the messages** you received, and the inspired actions you took.

Remember to stay flexible. The journey you are on doesn't have only one road to take, there are many, and often the road you didn't want to take is one that will inspire others you'll meet along the way. If it seems to be time to *turn left or right* – inquire again, and follow the next step given. This is about becoming more attuned to the many gifts we've been given, and the extraordinary gift you truly are.

CHAPTER 4

CREATING YOUR LIFE
WITH PURPOSE & LOVE

when the pulsation of divine Energy becomes the
guiding presence in your life… what once appeared
impossible… becomes probable…

Numerous books and teachers have emerged in the last few decades offering leading-edge understanding of ways to manifest our wants and dreams. *The law of attraction* became a global phenomenon; some saw it as a way to finally get whatever they had always felt was just out of reach – from loving relationships to dream-come-true careers – and some saw it as a tool solely for obtaining the material *things* of life. If you look at the timing of this dynamic, you can also see that it had an effect on the social norm – the victim attitudes of *Life just happens to me, I'm not in charge, and I can't do anything about it*. Many people began evolving from being at the mercy of their existence to being the cause of it, a paradigm shift that has far-reaching consequences as more of the world community realizes and fully accepts that *we can be responsible for generating our life circumstances and our future*.

creating from purpose and love
Initially, as often happens when deeply entrenched patterns are shifting, the pendulum swings too far. For many the focus became one of solely manifesting and obtaining more and more material possessions. We can invite, allow, and appreciate

all the prosperity life has to offer us, but if our only desire is for personal gain, we will be left feeling the futility of it all; empty and meaningless. Supportive, willing, benevolent contributions congruent with what you value and love are bastions of empowered creation. What is required to become fully empowered so that our lives reflect our inherent goodness – is to create from purpose and love.

The intellectual logical part of us that makes many of our life decisions hasn't the capacity to generate our greatest accomplishments, which are fueled by the creative heart/mind connection. This creative part of us is sourced by access to divine intelligence and has the ability and enthusiasm to create a future that reflects our highest aspirations.

The impulse arising today is to rediscover this knowledge, move beyond our illusory sense of powerlessness, and reconnect to the magnifying wisdom known by mystics, saints, sages, and shamans of ancient traditions in bygone eras.

amplifying the natural laws of attraction
with the energy of consciousness

Why now, why this time? We are in the midst of an evolutionary shift, where everything is in a process of advancement, but are we heading toward a sustainable future or a cataclysmic breakdown? To better comprehend the importance of our participation in creating our lives, the great Taoist master, Alfred Huang, translator of *The Complete I Ching*, the ancient Chinese oracle, has this to say:

'If we accept that every action we take is a cause that has an effect and every effect has a cause, we can more clearly see the results of our actions. The intention behind each action determines its effect. Our intentions and our actions affect not only ourselves but also others. If we believe that every intention and action evolves as we progress on our spiritual journey, then if we act consciously we evolve consciously, but if we act unconsciously we evolve unconsciously.[1']

If Light can be considered a container of information, then Love is the building block of creation. As the Energy of peace ignites conscious awareness it inspires new life circumstances to be developed. Your future is based on the choices you make, which in turn is dependent on your behavior and the actions you take in every moment. Learning to envision, dream, and create a future in harmony with your heart's intention isn't only for pioneers and inventors. You have access to the best partner possible, guidance from the universal principle of creation. Just by imagining what is possible you are magnifying the energy field that creates your reality.

dreaming and declaring your world into reality is so satisfying…
envisioning before 'doing' could become a natural habit
There is so much new and instinctive information coming to light now, figuratively and literally. Your inner life is more important than the *reality* that surrounds you; you can create whatever is meaningful to you. As you evolve, you find that you are suddenly cleaning out closets, giving away excess of any kind, eating simpler, choosing vacations that give you a greater sense of the culture and land you're visiting. Many people find their tastes become simplified, and are happiest just when enjoying each moment, wherever they are and with whatever they have. What has changed? It is the expansion of inner peace, offering you more contentment than any *thing* you ever purchased or did.

Inner purpose becomes a priority as you feel your heart wanting to be of service. You discover that working at certain jobs doesn't feel right anymore; you might leave them to search for work where you can apply the innate gifts you have to offer others. This is a journey of discovery; it doesn't happen overnight. As you walk toward this accelerated *inner knowing*, you have moments of fulfillment where nothing needs to be added to experience how truly magnificent life is.

setting new paradigms... the future

This is the time when you integrate all the knowledge you've gained and utilize the manifesting power of the Energy of consciousness to bring it into daily reality. As we evolve from the lower vibrations of bias, greed, and force, to align with principles of love, kindness, and compassion, we can set new paradigms in motion, and dream into existence a world that values all of humankind. In this chapter you will find stories of people who have transformed their lives through the power of their dreams and heart/mind visions. Individually and together, as we envision and take action on bringing a new way of BE-ing and living into existence, it will begin to happen – the fact that you are reading this book indicates that it has already begun.

Day by day, as you integrate higher learning inspired through time spent in Stillness, what emerges is a more loving, caring, and empowered you. At the end of this Chapter is The Practice, 'Making Requests' – it's an essential ingredient for creating your life and this world to be all that you have intended and dreamed. What better time than now to invite the deepest part of you to play on the inspired playground of your dreams.

FLIGHTS OF HOPE
in a remote location, miles from anywhere...
dreams can evolve that take us beyond known
boundaries, into skies of hope and promise...

He grew up on the plains of Africa, a Maasai – the renowned warriors of Kenya, many who live their lives today much as their forefathers have for centuries. He learned the ways of the land, carried a spear as a child, and was raised with the same cultural education as those of his tribe.

What is it that sets someone on a different track than their obvious heritage? Were the tests this young man faced those that gave him the conviction to change age-old traditions which affect the lives of every young boy growing up in his culture? Or was destiny at play here, an inner quest that would one day offer him a journey into the realization of his dreams? No matter how remote, even in the middle of a continent miles from anywhere, when it is your time – the gates open.

That entry into new worlds occurred on a moonlit night. It was providence; the crossroads where lives intersect to create pathways of hope for others whose dreams are yet to be realized. Cementing a friendship that would withstand drought, famine, political unrest, and sundry challenges that might have barred most people from ever believing in the impossible, Jackson's heart said hello even before he did. I met my new friend, *Action Jackson*, when a Maasai village became my home for the evening after the rains washed away the already unsuitable African roads that were to take me back to my lodge. A gracious invitation from my guide to stay in his village was truly impossible to turn down.

When the clouds parted, an opportunity arose to build a

campfire, and before long, there were countless warriors circling the blazing light. My guide surreptitiously announced that I could offer them a way to know that Stillness I spoke of – and *now* was a good time. The life force Energy of absolute peace Jackson experienced that night offered him insight that his life was about to change. For years he had dreamed of becoming a Maasai balloon pilot. Night after night he saw himself flying over the plains, showing people the magnificence of his land, and the rare animals that still roam the wild terrain.

His dream had a two-fold purpose. He intended to shift the tide of his people with regard to the infamous cultural practice of circumcision, first with boys, and then with girls – and he needed to make more money to fund this project, and all of his work at the clinic. Ballooning would bring in needed funds so he could continue this vital work.

Jackson's vision carried him through the most demanding of situations while attending hundreds of sick and destitute people at the clinic day after day. Only he had recently begun to lose the optimism that higher aspirations evoke. There were arduous and economic challenges at every turn, beyond what we can even imagine in the West. *Maybe his dreams were only lofty ideals, as many now joked.* Jackson had begun to feel pangs of hopelessness for the first time.

When I arrived at the clinic the day following the session, Jackson's eyes sparkled with the newfound happiness he felt. *"I'm beginning to understand…"* Jackson spoke of his depression in the previous months, when all that ran through his mind was, *"It's impossible. It's so much money."* But after the previous night's immersion into his true heritage and power, he believed with all his heart that his dream was meant to happen. He didn't know *how*, but he *knew* that it would.

This Maasai lived without borders in his mind; he lived a life of service – a visual essay of honesty, compassion, and goodness. But the road ahead would not be an easy one. I told him I would dedicate my next Stillness Session CD to support his dream and that we would stay in touch.

* * *

The next year was a time of political unrest; killings were rampant across Kenya and the drought added even more tension. Travel slowed, communication was cut off, and no tourists arrived, including friends from overseas who supported the clinic. When the phone lines finally worked, my dear friend spoke about the difficult time he was going through.

I told him about *trust,* the *knowing* that everything is working out for the best, even when you can't see it. Jackson was discovering this for himself; he knew the reason he hadn't gone to balloon school that year; many of the tribes had given him their consent and trust – and more than 137 circumcision ceremonies were performed. He needed to be there, they believed in him.

* * *

We continued to correspond whenever he could get an Internet connection. I tried to help him get a visa to go to flight school, but after 9/11, it was like running into a wall of *no's.* While I can't imagine too many terrorists flying around in balloons, it was just one more rationale why everyone believed it was *an impossible dream.* Everyone except Jackson – who continued asking the Universe to show him the best route to take.

The hope in Jackson's heart stayed strong, he told me how many of the Maasai's lives had been profoundly touched by their time in Stillness, and that seeing their transformation helped him to trust that his dream would also happen. The message he sent brought tears to my eyes, "*My life and Talek community have not been the same. We are optimistic about the future – and focused on our goals. And I am filled with hope.*" We continued to correspond; the next year I found a balloon school in California, and sent him the books he needed to begin his studies.

* * *

I had gotten used to living in a state of wonderment in those years, but when I awoke one morning to read an email with flight times of Jackson's arrival – it took my breath away. Jackson had left Africa! *And without even knowing if someone would be at the airport to pick him up!* Jackson had decided it was time for his dream to become real and trusted that it would.

Dreaming is not about being irresponsible, it's about being fully responsible for allowing your inner purpose to be realized, so you can love what you do and serve others along the way. When you have surrendered to a higher purpose, you invite the truly magical of life to appear.

This is the road to unconditional happiness. There is tremendous power when we are inspired to take action from our core values, the principles we share with all of humanity. That infinite peace and the awareness it offers makes the improbable – possible. Jackson began his balloon schooling and miraculously passed his first pilots' test, despite the obvious language barriers. I flew to California to meet with him, and invited a few people to get to know this beautiful soul as I had.

Friends of Jackson became a slogan for the extraordinary group who found themselves aboard this flight of hope. People could feel the generosity of his heart and it lit that passion within them. The power of his words, and the intention of his service resonated with such clarity that – in a grocery store, in line to get a cell phone, at picnics and film premieres, people asked to exchange phone numbers, to offer their homes, to plan fund-raising events, and on and on. He spoke at universities, observed surgeries at leading hospitals, taught school children about the Maasai tribe's culture, met with bankers and non-profit directors, gave numerous lectures wherever people would listen about circumcision and malaria – *and* learned how to surf, went fishing, played golf, and used a can opener – all for the first time.

Jackson's time in America touched many hearts, including his own. It was not always easy, for a long time, there was more love flowing than money, but he held onto his dream, and returned to the balloon school to complete his commercial pilot study and testing. And, he passed! The day after Christmas when Jackson went back to Africa, he took a lot of love and lifelong friendships with him.

Action Jackson's journey offered people a way to recognize their own dreams – how to create a life of purpose while loving your own. When you live connected to the power within your heart you can soar through the skies of your imagination as Jackson did so often, long before those flights above the plains of Africa became a reality. What can't we learn from the heart of one so pure? After all, soaring through skies of hope-filled dreams is our destiny as well…

In a world where our minds are often cluttered with vast amounts of information, distractions and complexity, we can easily lose our way. We forget that what ultimately brings us the most happiness is living with purpose.

- Write down your Requests of what you want to know.
- Listen to the Stillness Session recording

Answers will arrive at your door sooner than you can even imagine…

THE SOUND OF DESTINY KNOCKING

Cynicism is a magnificent quality to have in abundance if you want to ensure you remain asleep to the many gifts you're here to discover. It lived loud within my father as it does within many attorneys, judges, politicians, and countless people who have seen the underbelly of life, or just have lost their ability to dream or have hope in a future that inspires them. Neighbor Bob had lived his life with this misnomer, thinking it served him well, until the arrival of that elemental day when destiny's knock heralds a new beginning.

One afternoon, as the illustrious rays of a California sun began to wane, I set out for a walk in the hills encircling my new home. "Hello…" I waved. "Do you know of any good trails I can take around here?" My neighbor happened to be standing at his front door. "Sure," he replied. The man seemed distracted and rapidly relayed a variety of paths to hike the local hills and canyons.

On my return he was still standing in the doorway, but the look on his face had changed from curious to concerned. "I'm sorry if I seemed rude. I'm just worried about my wife. She went for a walk hours ago…" Just then a car pulled up, with friends who'd evidently been searching and seemed to have news. I felt sure he was in good hands and headed home.

* * *

A day later, I stopped by my neighbor's home to inquire if everything was okay. Bob's answer wasn't so much a request as a requirement: he and his dog Bull wanted to join me on my walk. When I asked about his wife, the story behind the tense smile spilled out. "My wife drinks. In the beginning of my marriage I thought it would be fine, but it isn't. She passed out in the woods. They found her face-down."

This very hurt and worried man needed someone to listen, to hear the cry buried in his heart that wanted to come screaming into the light of day. It's what you haven't expressed because part of you feels like it's not real until the day arrives when it hurts too much to hold it in anymore. I understand that pain, the one that alcoholism and addiction of any kind inflicts on the lives of everyone it touches. Whether you're the addict or it's a member of your family, it's devastating. You think you can help, that you can change the person, but it's a never-ending spiral that *never* reaches bottom.

When I assured him that he would be able to find the best answers for himself and for his wife; he responded sharply. His sadness turned into razor-sharp cynicism. "You don't really believe that stuff you write on your website, do you?"

Bob had obviously done homework on his new neighbor. The look on his face was like a large-print news headline, "*You must be out of your ____ mind!!*" And yet, what lay beneath his words was a sense of painful resignation – that feeling of reaching a road that goes nowhere – and wanting it to be different with all your heart, wanting life to *not* be the way it is.

He stopped walking. The cross-examination continued in even greater angst, "So why did that happen for you? Why not me? *Why not me*??"

* * *

Standing in the middle of an empty road, with no thought other than to do what comes naturally so this man could recognize the knowing was within him as well – I placed my hand on his arm. Breathing deep… the rhythmic pulsation of that boundless Energy captured the heart and mind of the one seeking that innate power within his soul. I could literally feel that formless vibration as it became corporal, and moved from an internal flame of consciousness through the structure of his entire body. His eyes flashed in recognition. No words were spoken. Moments like these demonstrate what it means for *time to stand still*. It doesn't matter what you believe or understand to be true – when that transmission of what is truly timeless knocks at the door, your life undergoes a profound change. It's just that simple.

I left for a tour of Africa soon after that day. What I didn't know was that Bob hadn't drawn a flickering flame, but a brightly blazing bonfire that was propelling him to discover what had happened on that road. Whatever it was, he knew he wanted more.

Bob called the office using his neighborly skills to get a not-yet-published Stillness Session audio. He later shared that on early morning walks, listening to *Dawn of a New Day* as the sun rose on the horizon, reignited a passion for living that had seemed irreparably damaged. This once hardened cynic's shell fell away, into the sands of time where he continued releasing the habitual negativity that hadn't allowed him to know the loving brilliance of his true nature.

* * *

A roller coaster of *awakening* placed him front and center; feeling exuberant one moment, and on a downward slide the next. His wife's drinking had been in existence for the full ten years of their marriage and nothing he did had changed the excessive way she treated her health. Now that his blinders were off, Bob could see what he hadn't before. He took the steps needed to get a divorce, all the while trying to discover how to be aligned with the new Bob that didn't want to be hurtful – even when he felt like striking back. *Making Requests* became his game of choice, informing him how to be fair and supportive, without being taken advantage of and without taking on her problems as though they were his.

It was *the best of times and the worst of times* as the saying goes and Bob's life was in full measure of its meaning. This nonbeliever of anything even slightly spiritual discovered a heart filled with love. A quality of strength resonated within him, supporting the dark hours when the trials of divorce filled his mind with the '*if only* syndrome *– if only I had known better*'.

But the messages he heard in Stillness inspired him to do the uncommon, not only during the challenges of his divorce, but in making decisions for a new future. He listened and allowed the guidance he received to direct his life. Rather than immediately find a new home, he decided to take a road trip, get re-acquainted with his parents and friends that he hadn't seen in years.

Three days after he left his parents home, he got a call from his father. His mother had unexpectedly passed in the night! She hadn't even been ill. Bob was awestruck by the grace that had orchestrated these final days with his mother, where he got to know and love her more than ever. How could you plan anything as sublime as this? You can't. You learn to trust and listen, and allow the synchronicity of life to unfold as perfectly as it always does.

By the end of the trip my good neighbor realized he really didn't have any more ties to California. Even though he felt he couldn't earn a good living in Taos, Bob packed up and moved cross-country. After finding *un chiquita casa* that was even *mas fabuloso* than his much loved last home, he settled in to meet new friends and search for work in a town that's famous for having none, or at least, none that might pay him what he needed to live.

Amazing grace struck again. Being the visionary he was, Bob purchased a domain in the early days of the Internet, and had literally forgotten about it when he received a call from someone wanting to own it. He couldn't believe it! And it gave him the financial resources to do what his heart always dreamed: play music. In this moment, it wasn't about *making it big* – it was about the simple pleasures of life.

Once Bob grasped the infinite nature of all that had happened over the last year, he understood what truly satiates our hunger. It is to continually create life from the guidance that offers us pathways to happiness. Cynicism is a word that no longer describes my dear friend Bob... he's now a man who relishes each moment as the gift it is – and the gift he truly has become.

The Life Circumstances Model clarifies the progression of the healing process – from developing conscious choices to generating new life circumstances. Review where you are in this cycle and what steps you would like to take that will generate outcomes in harmony with your Intentions.

- Listen to the Stillness Session Recording.
- Make Requests.
- Contemplate your experiences. Allow them to inform your actions and behavior.
- Write down your insights. And smile...

STEP BY STEP

Dreams begin as thoughts... Since we think many in the day, they don't become REALITY until we create a structure where they can exist. Some foundations are built on sand... soon they give way.

Step by Inspired Step, Thought by Inspired Thought, Action by Inspired Action forms the base... of a FOUNDATION that can sustain your DREAM...

Everything you aspire to bring into existence is possible, when you say so...

Request, Listen, and Allow your dreams to come true... and before long... they truly do

MAKING REQUESTS

requests are powerful magnets combining the magnified
potency of intention with the humility and eloquence of
prayer and grace

Now that the principles of Energy into matter have begun
to define new possibilities, how can you bring more of the
power of this creative force into your life? *Making Requests*
is the ultimate creation process, entraining the quantum field
of all information, that library of boundless, brilliant wisdom
to coalesce with the power of intention. With the release of
pre-existing conditioning, and the heightened awareness that
arrives as you connect with this evolutionary dimension of
consciousness, your search includes not only manifesting the
material things of life but creating all of it with purpose and
love.

Making Requests are a principal form of bringing the
profound, the practical, and the providential into existence.
They are not demands or fervent pleas, but a comprehensive
approach for combining directed quantum energy potential
with ancient wisdom. Requests are made in a form of humility
or prayer, as one would when approaching the wisdom of
Truth, whether by name to a higher power – or nameless –
nature in its purest form. Being humble is a virtue to cultivate
throughout one's life, as it is a teacher of equality and respect,
and carries with it an attitude that is receptive to the possibility
of overcoming all difficulties.

When you request guidance, you invite the natural laws of

universal attraction to respond. Electromagnetic fields within us broadcast this focused and intentional communication not only to the *intelligent* cells within the body, but also out into the *listening* Universe where the quantum sea manifests all energy forms (thoughts) into matter.

I am constantly amazed at how something as seemingly simple as *Making a Request* consistently works. Whenever I am at a loss for what to do in any situation, taking the time to focus and write down my Request for even greater clarification always brings new insights. Fears dissipate when you have answers to what you believe are impossible situations. The more evidence you have of how simply you are able to access inspired solutions, the more you learn to trust and believe that grace is always there.

In this chapter, 'Creating Your Life With Purpose & Love', both Jackson and Bob discovered for themselves, time and again when in *impossible* situations, that the opening to the profound mysteries of life occurred by *Making Requests,* bringing answers they might not have ever considered.

When you recognize that what you ultimately want is what's best for all concerned, then it's easy to frame your Requests in a different form than when you *ask* for something to go your way at all costs. If you were having difficulties with a member of your family, would you ask to win the argument *no matter what*? Or would you want to know how to take care of every person you are in relationship with in the most respectful way? I've included here a few samples from my personal journal, made during a difficult time when my mother was in a coma and my sister and I were not in agreement of how to take care of her:

- **Please bring me** a greater recognition of how my sister and

I can stand united in our decisions at this challenging time.
- **Please show me** the best way, the most loving way, to take care of my mother with strength and knowing and will.
- **Please allow** what my mother needs to become clear – so I can assist her in this time of transition.

Writing Your Requests

Writing down your Requests increases their potency by concentrating the focus of your intention. Once you release expectations of the outcome, you open to whatever the Universe wants to offer, which is often appreciably better than what you requested. The answers emerge seemingly out of nowhere. You could easily forget you ever even made the Request, which is why writing in a journal is so important to give your mind the evidence it needs to make practices like this the principal centered habits that motivate and form your actions.

The Practice of Making Requests:

- **Reflect** on where you would like to have more understanding. What you want for yourself and/or others – from loving relationships to meaningful careers, from financial well-being to health and vitality, to creating solutions for what could appear to be hopeless and dire challenges.
- **Write a specific Request** regarding this point in your journal.
- **Listen to the Stillness Session CD.** As you connect with that infinite creative principle, invite the inspiration that offers unimagined answers.
- **Listen** for the messages or insights that could arise at this time.
- **Allow** in the knowing that everything happening is in your best interest to align you with your life's purpose and a

quality of living that attracts greater love and prosperity.

- **Write the answers** of what actions to take, including doing nothing (non-action) in this moment. Remember that answers can appear later in the week, so continue to write down whatever inspiration arises, and follow through.

This Week's Practice:

- **Write one Request** wherever you're feeling challenged, whether in your personal life or business.
- **Use The Three Breath Awareness** to invite inspiration. Continue with the instructions above.
- **Use the Stillness Session CD** later in the week. Each connection to infinite intelligence reveals new answers. Continue integrating relevant practices.

Next week make the Request about a dream or a vision where you want more insight. While it's helpful to always write your Requests, they can be made anywhere, anytime. By putting your attention on what you truly want guidance with, simply speak or think your Request to bring it into greater focus.

There is comfort and security in knowing we are always guided and loved. What you learn from this practice – and your commitment to it – can release the confusion that causes suffering and replace it with an aliveness and appreciation for all of life. Then all that is left to do... is smile... knowing that answers are on the way.

CHAPTER 5

CROSSING THE THRESHOLD – LETTING GO OF OLD STRUCTURES

some of life's most incredible moments arrive when we finally let go... allowing something we never thought possible to emerge

As we all know, for every door closing, there is one opening... and every ending... heralds a new beginning. When you take that first step energetically in the direction of your highest aspirations, you will often encounter many things that no longer *feel right* to you anymore, i.e., constrictive thoughts, ideas, beliefs, relationships, jobs, and even clothes that no longer align with who you've become.

You could discover that books or movies you used to think were exciting or fun – just aren't enjoyable anymore, especially if they were violent. This is a natural consequence of releasing old patterns that resonate with the lower energies of anger, cruelty, drugs, alcohol, and fear, as you begin acquiring new ones that resonate with the higher vibrational energy of light-heartedness, thoughtfulness, acceptance, and appreciation.

Consider how nature in its purest sense is in a state of cooperation with the earth energetically. This is what is happening to humanity as we begin to *vibrate* on higher levels of consciousness. Many people find they suddenly choose healthier foods to eat, no longer drink excessive amounts of alcohol, and want to surround themselves with happier, more loving and kind people in their personal relationships, as well as at their place of work.

Everyone's process is unique, and it's important to honor this unfolding in your life by listening to the guidance from that inner teacher who is always ready to lead the way. I am not suggesting that you make radical massive shifts immediately where you're left feeling upside down. And yet, if the structures surrounding you that have given you a sense of security begin crumbling – you could have reached that momentous marker, where the only real choice you have is to *cross the threshold* into the new life that awaits you – sooner than later. As unnerving as this might seem, once you follow the signals, a whole new world of possibility appears. The stories in this book are filled with people who heard the calling. And this chapter includes those who learned to listen and followed the messages they *heard*. What you'll discover, just as they did, is that where you're heading is immeasurably greater than what you've known.

crossing the threshold

Crossing the threshold appeared for me as a crisis of conscience. I could no longer live with decisions I had previously made that were influencing every part of my life. And even though I couldn't imagine a future different than the one I thought I would have – *I had to step into that new world*. I had to take that leap of faith regardless of my fears, because my conscience – or was it my consciousness – was now speaking louder than all my doubts. We always have a choice in life, but in this moment, I felt I had only one, and if I didn't make it, I could no longer live with myself.

Crossing that threshold is about releasing self-imposed

limitations. For many, it is a life-changing experience, where infinite intelligence propels you to *let go* of your present situation, which could appear to be a comfortable existence, although at closer inspection it is often an empty one – to step boldly into a new future. These are the pivotal moments of realization that compel us to *die* to old ways of being so that we can ultimately be reborn. We are being called to release the conditioning that has held us bound, so we can allow a deeper truth to emerge. This time of letting go entreats us to trust in the absolute intelligence of the infinite, which is an essential element in discovering the mystery of what we at one time inherently knew.

learning to trust

My life experiences had taught me there were very few people I could trust. The conscious awareness that opened through the Energy field of absolute peace gave me every reason to trust. I learned that each time I *leapt into the unknown* what would unfold in the coming days or months would always be better than the plans I had made. People think I am courageous, but I am simply listening to the inherent *knowing* that has shown me time and again where the true magic of life exists. Once you get this... you would be foolish to respond in any other way.

Living with this level of trust invites you to step forward, to act from the inner courage that has now revealed itself – instead of the programming that has kept humanity cynical, guarded, and complacent, hiding in the shadows of the mind. This level of trust activates unique forms of communication. You hear yourself speaking in ways that are more fully aligned with your soul's purpose. It all begins so simply, with just being willing to *let go* and take that first step into your new life.

let the magic begin

You can't experience the joy of being fully alive when you hold onto anything – whether it's the past, people, or regrets of any kind. In this chapter are stories of people who found the courage to release their doubts, and cross the threshold into a life that was in harmony with their heart/mind intention and highest principles. At the end is the Practice that supports you to blaze a path of your own self expression and a life filled with optimism and true happiness.

THE ELUSIVE DREAM

"I've worked hard for this. I don't understand how they can even ask me! What am I supposed to do?" His words were like the anguished cry of a battle-weary peacekeeper watching his dreams slowly and surely slip into mists of oblivion. My cynical, intellectual, often arrogant, yet endearing, and always good-hearted friend was really up against it now.

Jake had chosen to set his latest aspirations on producing an *impossibly challenging* documentary, a story of great strength and stamina, owned by an equally powerful and strong-willed man. He had spent months working without pay to bring this elusive project some reality and had succeeded until, quite unexpectedly, he received an ultimatum to accept a lesser *producing credit* or '… get nothing and just walk away'. The smoke and illusion of titles, especially in the domain of Hollywood grandiosity, can create a reality that opens doors to offers and projects where none exist. Jake's outcries were those that arrive from the depth of a man's heart when he believes that he won't be able to play on the field of dreams he knows is his birthright.

show me the money... or at least the fame

It had been drilled into Jake his whole life that hard work would take him to the top of that ladder of recognition and success, and that putting in endless hours of work would create the results he envisioned. We've all been there, endlessly slaving away when we're not conscious of how to be the architects of our own lives. Many Eastern traditions describe unconsciousness as humanity's inability to see beyond the *veil* – that thin layer of deception that holds Truth just beyond sight – where we have forgotten our inherent *knowing,* our ability to access that Energy sea that creates all of life.

How Jake *viewed* this event would be the game changer – more than the *facts* or *reality* of what was happening. The universe is all too happy to give us what we believe. If Jake believed all was lost – it would be. If he believed his dreams would always evade him – they would. And, if even in the midst of adversity, he could learn to trust that what was happening would ultimately benefit him – anything could happen.

the game changer

What to do? Jake didn't need the title to create his dreams – that was another illusion. "What do you *really* want?" I invited him to take a deeper look. Jake's fervent response was, "I want to make a film that touches people's hearts to recognize their humanity. *And* I want my title! I earned it! Why should I give it up!?!" His words reverberated the indignity he felt.

Jake could create a reality beyond the one that was unfolding. Accessing the inherent power within is the game changer. His struggle was one many live with, because you can't transform what you're not aware of. We must first gain the strength to be with any pain that might surface as we become conscious. It's only then these hidden purveyors of suffering that have been too traumatic to see or deal with – can be dissolved.

"What can I do?!?" Jake's outburst was an enduring cry for 'the powers that be' to show the way.

"If you insist on keeping your title now, will the film get made?"

"No." The only thing Jake could see clearly now was anger and defeat. He had the right to the title. Yet, if he fought for it, his life would be mired in waging a war of endless battles.

becoming present and letting go

When you let go of beliefs that bind you, what appears is beyond your imagination. Infinite intelligence reveals the underlying principles of form into matter; thoughts manifesting into events become evident as you see the un-manifest becoming reality over time. This equation was evidenced when answers to Jake's questions surfaced during a Stillness Session one serendipitous night. Embittered states were left behind, answers received, and limitations that had been thought real were dissolved.

Jake had a vision of himself as a young child, longing for his father's love and approval. He saw the boy who continued to ask for tenderness, even after being knocked unconscious from his chair at the dining table. Jake watched as the child who wanted assurance that he was *worthy* of being loved, returned again and again, beseeching his dad to give him that message of security and comfort. He never got it.

What he saw were the many ways the brokenhearted child kept looking, in one situation after the next throughout his entire life. Beneath the fractured layers of loss and grief, what his vision uncovered brought him a new resolve. He didn't have to look any further. The cry welling up inside him was now one of liberation, "*I am that love I've wanted to find…*"

Words are a form of *illumination* not only by what they express, but through the vibrational content of the Light they transmit. What Jake shared opened the heart of everyone who heard it. The room resounded in sacred Stillness, the kind you feel in the inner sanctum of spaces where whispered prayers echo a call to the infinite. This power exists within everyone when you speak from a place of purity – even your mind won't be able to question what you experience when it's as palpable as what this force emits. It allows you to let go ever so gently of anything that holds you back, and the immeasurable Energy of peace that streams forth generates improbable dreams into existence.

What you envision is greatly impacted once you know how to access this field of potential, this pulsing stream of life. It's not about stressing, efforting, or working hard. It's about taking action from inspiration. And, an amazing gift of this knowledge is that you become happy with what you *already* have. So, you play the game, no longer feeling anxious, but rather as a way to take responsibility for your life, seeing it as an adventure and blessing. In a moment of recognition, the newly enlightened man-without-a-title was given everything he needed to make the decision. Jake released the beliefs that had bound his situation in complete despair, called the film's director and relinquished the title that had once held so much meaning.

Within 24 hours the quantum field of potential where his thoughts had gone began to create the impossible. The director was so impressed with the courage it had taken for Jake to let go of his position after all he had done to get the film made, that he recommended him to a film-maker who had just lost her producer. The director suggested she do everything in her power to hire Jake. He told her how fortunate she would be to work with a person who had a level of integrity not often found in this business where deceit and despair live like brothers from the same family.

Jake tried to act low-key when he called, but the euphoria in his voice was indicative of the story he had to share. He got the job! And on a film he felt deeply passionate about – a documentary about children with greater challenges than most of us will ever have to face – living without parents, without knowing they are loved, and living with the reality their days are numbered from the disease of AIDS.

The film completely matched Jake's vision; it was a declaration of hope and inspiration in a sea of uncertainty, a penetrating perspective of mortality and transcendence. And, he could give these kids the love that was now pouring out of him. Jake was booked on a flight for Africa, leaving in just two weeks. And – oh, by the way – this project had that elusive title attached to it. He would be credited as the producer of the film.

* * *

Beyond what fame and fortune can ever offer, what Jake received was the richest gift of all, the awareness at the depth of his being, that he is loved. So much opens in your life when you *really* get this. Now, the titles would come and so would the fortune. It's just the way it is. Jake won numerous awards in the years ahead, including the highest accolades possible from Amnesty International.

His unwavering vision produced more films of a world united in a common value of respect for all humanity. Jake's life began to model the dream he had envisioned – the one that truly resonated with his heart. What more could you ever want than that? If one day you see Jake's smiling face receiving an Oscar, you can smile right back, as you now know the road there, and how to take it for yourself.

THE SUITCASE

The word *exploration* takes on new meaning when you have given agreement, somewhere in the innermost sanctum of your soul that you are ready – to cross whatever threshold is needed, to find that seemingly ever-distant illuminating peace within. When Morgan said she wanted to photograph and document the Stillness Programs I'd be offering the Dogon tribe in Mali, Africa, I'm sure she never expected, after all her years traveling the globe for *National Geographic*, just how uniquely memorable the journey would be. This time, it wasn't about the cultures she would visit, the art of travel, or the bliss one imagines a spiritual pilgrimage might invoke. Where this exploration took her was beyond any notions of grace arriving on the wings of a dove, into the reality of a 21st-century wake-up call.

This exceptionally talented, self-reliant journalist had traveled through 40 countries during Communist occupation, ridden yaks across Mongolia, and traversed through China when most people thought it too dangerous. She knew how to handle the most challenging situations with ease, and yet, in this moment, Morgan had become like a child whose favorite blanket had been snatched from her. In hundreds of thousands of miles traveled, it had never happened – not once. Morgan's suitcase was lost – with odds set never to see again.

How would it ever reach us? If found, it would have to be hand-carried to an airline that would take it to Casablanca, on to Bamako and after that, hand-carried again to another airline going to Mopti. Even if it made it that far, we would be traveling daily to new locations. The possibility of retrieving it was slim, very slim. Morgan's eyes shot arrows of anger at a world that had rendered her helpless – or so it seemed.

Choosing this time to speak to someone about how they must break the pattern they are in before it can turn around is really not the best idea. There is just no access to possibility when you're in an anxious or angry frame of mind. And, this is *exactly when* you must find a way to release your negative emotions if you want an outcome other than the one that is about to occur.

The laugh lines that normally appeared at the edge of Morgan's eyes had disappeared. What she wanted was reassurance that what seemed completely out of her control – wasn't. We've all been there before, shouting at the world and everyone in it, how life *just isn't fair*. Morgan knew there was something to be gleaned from this situation, and it infuriated her that she didn't 'get' what it was.

* * *

We all have a choice; it's called free will. Once we become present and accept *what is* – we can shift our emotional (vibrational) state and from here tap into the inspiration of what to do next. Or we can rage against our current situation, and life becomes one of *re-action* to the chaos that suddenly seems to surround us everywhere – whether it's at home, at work, or the streets of Mopti, Africa. Morgan had been on the evolutionary train long enough to know everything could transform in a second. This was clearly not going to happen now, as disappointment coupled with the exhaustion of 30 hours of travel, had completely taken this memory from her.

Resistance of any kind keeps us in a stuck world where nothing changes. One tragic story leads to the next. Breakfast arrived and as the delectable dark chocolate began to melt her fury, Morgan began moving back into resourcefulness. She started journaling visions of anything that could make the days ahead easier, and of the miraculous arrival of her suitcase. Recognizing that we can choose how we feel is the golden key that frees us from suffering. And, when we create anew from that higher vibration of acceptance, events are drawn to us from the field of potential where the uncommon and extraordinary exist.

The moment Morgan's venomous state left her – the phone rang. The man at the luggage counter in London had found her bag and was putting it on a flight to Casablanca himself. Her luggage would arrive tomorrow. Oh happy day!! Happy, happy, happy day!! The laugh lines returned with a grin that spoke volumes.

* * *

But the lesson wasn't complete, and so the elusive luggage continued on its journey, getting stopped in myriad locations. By day five, the world traveler had had enough. Our Dogon guide did his very best, but the suitcase seemed to be part of a fantastical story that always ended in taking *one more day* to arrive. Similar to an unconscious pattern, nothing shifted. A flat tire on the road to Djenne was the reminder needed to now begin *physically* moving that *stuck-ness* out.

In the middle of nowhere – nothing around for miles, no houses, no people, just desert brush and red plains as far as the eye could see – Morgan let it out. "Aarghhhhhhh...

Aarghhhhhhh!!!" Again and again she railed against everything she considered unjust, everything that angered, upset, or infuriated her; it was clearly no longer about the suitcase. And the powerful compassionate wind howling in sympathy across the Mali desert dissolved it all into the dusty ethers now swirling around us.

It's not easy to release what we don't know exists, which is why becoming conscious is crucial to eliminating suffering. Our guide Mikaelu couldn't stop laughing. He was after all, a Dogon, and the ancient knowledge of his lineage had taught him much that we in the Western world need to learn about living in harmony with ourselves, the universe, and each other.

* * *

The tire was fixed – the tire that blew at the perfect time to assist a fellow traveler on her true journey. As we all climbed back into the jeep – the phone rang. This time it was for sure. Morgan's luggage was safe and only a few miles away. Remarkable? Wondrous? Likely? How is it possible, considering all the different airlines, countries, customs, and languages this baggage had to go through, that it could have found its way back to its owner? Once Morgan released the agitation she was experiencing, and was no longer sending out signals that matched how she felt – the way opened.

And yet, the greatest miracle of all was not about the safe passage of luggage. It wasn't about incompetent airlines or living with discomfort. It was about Morgan's *deepest wish*, to live each day connected to who she is at her very core. To find that, we have to become present to each moment as it is. We might even have to lose something along the way.

Sometimes grace is as elegantly simple as losing a suitcase.

And getting it back becomes part of the unfolding of one person's journey to living in connection to the greatest gift of all... how to Be in each moment, with the recognition of who you truly are beyond it... accepting the power you have to then transform it...

When you first wake up... Listen... What thoughts are there? Are they ones you want to carry into the day? If not, now could be a good time to do The Three Breath Awareness.

Release unconscious thoughts that don't support you and create new ones... that inspire and empower your life. Now is a good time to begin your day...

THE CALL TO ADVENTURE

Their first call to adventure must have arrived when the young missionaries decided to share their love of God with the Polynesians on a remote island in Tahiti. I imagine they never expected the adventure to take them quite where it did, and yet... they were listening.

As I stepped onto the deck, the quiet of the early morning spoke to me. What I heard was that it was a perfect time to *dive* in the Stillness that is always inviting me to slow down. I asked the host of my bungalow to join me in listening to my first recording of a Stillness Session. He was curious to know if he might bring along the two missionaries who had stopped by for coffee on this chilly, overcast morning. His suggestion was quite interesting, considering that he had mentioned, only a day ago, how disturbed he was by their proselytizing. *What a fascinating day this was going to be.*

The missionaries, my host, and I all sat on the deck overlooking the windswept charcoal sea. The recording began, intermittently fluctuating from very soft to quite loud. *Why were there sound problems? It was a new recording. How could that be?* The engineer had just given it to me when I left for the airport. When the sound didn't improve, I wondered if I should look for another system it could be played on. As bad as that recording was – by now everyone was probably feeling more irritated than anything else.

When I looked in their direction, what I saw amazed me.

Everyone's eyes were closed; their faces revealed what they were experiencing, and it was anything but displeasure – quite the opposite. How was it possible that even with an unintelligible recording and bad acoustics, the alchemy of divine peace was being conveyed through the Stillness Session CD? The Universe seemed to be using every situation I found myself in – to teach me, and this incident was no exception. The transcendent Energy that had skyrocketed its presence into my life was showing me how simply it could convey *the goods* to whoever was ready to take the ride. Energy is, after all, a form of 'soundless' communication that transmits much like sound waves travel through the ocean, the earth, and the atmosphere. Obviously, it could cross any apparent barriers to touch the hearts of those ready to listen.

The recording played on. The winds gently cooled us from the sun, which had just broken through the clouds. Light was streaming across the endless blue of the horizon. I only saw it briefly as I closed my eyes to join them in that fathomless world of absolute tranquility.

The younger of the two missionaries opened his eyes slowly when the Session ended. He spoke of the experience as one of deep tranquility. One he recognized from special moments quietly looking out over the breathtaking beauty of the wilderness near his home. He was at once thoughtful and then quite animated as he spoke of his life passion, which was to be a politician. "I want to create solutions for making this a better world." His words were colored by the enthusiasm of a visionary speaking the dream of his future into existence. "I believe it's possible. I just don't think people ever really hear each other anymore."

During the rest of the time we spent together on that memorable morning he didn't speak of anything that created a divide between him and our host. All that was left for this trailblazer of a new world to share was the kindred light of his own heart.

* * *

The missionary from Polynesia hadn't spoken a word. On his face was the look of someone who has just tasted the wonders within and is left speechless. I know that look; it's when we have no words to describe the colors that now flood our world with new sensations and feelings. Once we discover how much we don't know, the way there can expand. I asked my host to translate.

"Can you speak English?"

"Only very little."

"Did you understand what I said on the CD?"

"Only very little."

"Something happened, didn't it? Would you like to tell us?"

The experience hadn't left him. The dark-skinned missionary, who looked like an athlete with his massive build, had the most tender look on his face. And even though he spoke in a language that was unknown to me, I could *feel* everything he was sharing.

"My mind became very still. Suddenly, there was so much light... It was coming from inside me... and going out from me to the world..." Silence overtook him once again. What is there to say, when you first come to know that you are so much more than what you thought? The gentleness emanating from this big Polynesian said it all. In the Stillness of being, no words are needed. What he shared was the goodness of his soul. The words he spoke swept over us like a wave of reverence when one realizes the depth to which we are loved.

In this moment, created by the essence that lies within us all, anything that might have caused separation, such as religion, culture, or beliefs, melted in the space of pure presence. The harmonic convergence of what lies beyond the sounds we can hear, is what defines the unity that Love will always orchestrate. Play on, dear conductor. Play on... and on... and on.

THE STILLNESS THAT ANSWERS PRAYERS

Letting go of what doesn't serve you can be as simple as... seeing what it is... getting clarity that you no longer wish to host this habit... and releasing it in the Stillness that answers prayers...

And it can be as challenging as... believing there is nothing to let go of... and living in the illusion that it's so...

It is in this moment... you can choose.

BECOMING PRESENT & LETTING GO
when you create space for what you truly love
to enter your life... it does

In this chapter, 'Crossing the Threshold', we explored the process of *Becoming Present*, being conscious of what exists, and *Letting Go*, releasing restrictive beliefs to make space for a new dimension to enter your life. This dynamic process shapes and forms your ability to live from your greatest potential.

Letting go of behaviors or patterns that have been detrimental to your overall happiness can be quite challenging. Anytime we release something, it naturally creates a void. Many mistake this space as an unwanted emptiness, but really it's just a blank canvas where a new world is ready to be created. Rather than fear this void, you could befriend it. Each old habit you replace with a healthier one creates an opening for the invisible world of conscious Energy to become more verifiable.

Another form of letting go is giving yourself permission to become still and *do nothing*. Our modern culture of constant *doing* is a natural inhibitor to creating spaciousness. Knowing when not to *get it done* instigates time to tap into the source of true power where solutions to challenges and the inspiration to create your dreams – are actually more accessible and immediate – over spinning endlessly in negativity and confusion.

inspired action and non-action
What if every action was taken from the inspiration you receive when connected to a universal field of intelligence?

Just consider the difference that would make in your life. Most people live in a constant state of reaction. When you're in that life stream of all knowing, you connect with people who want to be helpful, need less time to accomplish your work, discover the best routes to stay out of traffic, and on and on. Connecting to the source of your power *before* taking action transforms even the basic tenets of living.

When I was in film production, my business partner would sometimes arrive at work frustrated and worried, with a long list of calls to make. He didn't realize that you rarely get the response you're hoping for when you're not flowing with that stream of conscious awareness, and that he would actually garner more negative feedback than positive when the person he reached connected energetically with his anxious vibration.

Initially, people have a difficult time understanding this – as that big To Do List can seem so *insistent and demanding*. Morgan's resistance to her situation inhibited her access to move forward with fluidity and ease. Jake and the missionaries were initially in a rigid mindset that doesn't support entry to inspiration or heart-to-heart communication. When swirling activity and challenges surround you, the best, and first thing to do is – *become present*. Shifting your emotional state is more important than crossing something off that proverbial list.

Often, the best thing *to do* is... *nothing at all*, allowing space for inspiration by leaving a void. It is here, in this essential *non-doing*, where you release attachment to the outcome – that the miraculous emerges to show you a different pathway for getting where you want to go. You can't tap into the Energy field of inspired solutions or discover the unforeseen if you are always racing to *get it done* at all costs.

When my partner took action from inspiration, he would be

guided to wait until a more propitious time – and miraculous events would ensue. Inspired action shifts everything.

The Practice of Becoming Present & Letting Go:
- **Become Present by using The Three Breath Awareness –** Slow everything down.
- **Let Go** of whatever is energetically blocking you in this moment by taking a walk, going to the gym, or watching a film until you feel an emotional and physical release.
- **Become still. Be in the creative void of inaction.**
- **Reflect on what wants to be revealed, allow any emotions to be released, and Write the awareness in your journal.**

This Week's Practice:
- **Make a list of whatever prevents you from being your greatest self.** Write it in your journal. Contemplate what your life would feel like if you no longer had these influences.
- **Listen to the Stillness Session recording.** Ask for assistance to release anything that is blocking you, and allow the coming week to present you with new insights.
- **Write down the inspiration** you receive now and during the week. You don't have to let go all at once of every habit or behavior that isn't working. Slowly, naturally, step by step. Remember it's a journey… you have time.
- **Actively commit to letting go** of one concern, fear, or negative attribute that no longer serves the empowered you. No matter how big or small, just commit to letting it go. Feel what it's like for the empowered you to consciously respond to whatever life challenges appear.

CHAPTER 6

TRIALS AND TRIBULATIONS...
& OTHER BUMPS ON THE ROAD

when you dare life to be incredible there will always be
a series of challenges that arise...

Life is filled with trials and tribulations, and when you haven't integrated your connection to higher guidance, your troubles, like bad habits, cycle endlessly. When walking a road of transformation, they appear as signals; and as you become aware of what they represent, you no longer have to carry them into your future. Whatever difficulties you are facing now that might appear insurmountable, could have appeared to help you gain clarity of the (unconscious) source of your pain, and your strength to overcome it.

It would be lovely to think we could somehow bypass these *troublesome* times, and yet they are the events that can bring the greatest insights. As outdated concepts burn in the fires of illumination that heightened awareness offers, the wisdom we are given can be likened to Helen Keller's cognitive state when suddenly *knowing* there was life beyond the darkness she had lived in for years.

a time of profound change
We all have hurdles to conquer at different stages of our evolution. The good news is that we are living at a time when anything that conceals the light of our true nature is being brought to the surface so that it can be healed. When you have

reunited with your soul's deepest knowing, you'll understand how the events that molded your life were *determined* for the very purpose of guiding you into higher consciousness.

Once this limitless Energy ignites within, it's like being offered a free pass to the best rides at the park. There is often total exhilaration as your energetic field defines new life events where you ride on a magical expressway – and then, there is that lull between the highs when an elementary recognition of just how much you don't know appears. The way forward is dimly lit and yet it is directly ahead. Will you leave the security of your previous *safe harbor* to reach this new sphere of awareness? This is the ground that builds the inner strength, courage, and wisdom to battle the *ego-self* that consistently lashes out for control at all costs to your transformation.

When difficulties arise it's important to recognize that these events are not who *you* are. Nor do they have anything to do with the person you are blaming – not the spouse, lover, or friend who disappoints you, or the parents or family members who aren't able to offer you what you want. Everyone is just playing the *role* that aids you in reaching the promise of all that you have truly wanted; freedom from suffering and knowing unbounded Love. Whenever you feel triggered by an unresourceful emotion that plays into your being a victim, become still and connect with that limitless dimension, where you perceive what exists beneath the surface of the turmoil.

everything is unfolding perfectly

We learn from everyone, whether they are people we consider friends or adversaries. In this chapter, you will often find that times of greatest conflict where people had to contend with the most antagonistic individuals were junction points that had far-reaching consequences. They always accelerated each person's ability to assimilate higher learning and to shift the status quo.

One thing you can be assured of, you are never given a situation you can't handle. *When you recognize that everything that transpires is to bring you benefit, even if you can't see it immediately – you will understand more clearly what living an empowered life is all about.* That stream of grace that exists in all moments will have become a living presence in your life, not conceptually, but in reality.

One day you'll notice that you don't handle upsets in the same way you did before; the bumps in the road seemed to have smoothed out with the thoughts that you now keep, that resonate energetically with your inner conviction. As your foundation becomes stronger, you become confident you can handle any challenges that might arise. A well of courage, strength, love, and acceptance exists within you, just waiting to become your everyday experience – when this happens, trials and tribulations will no longer concern you; they will just be the markers that bring you even more awareness of the amazing life you now lead.

THE BUILDING

Some of our habits and beliefs are so ingrained we don't even know we have them until someone points them out, and then we often try to deny them. It was the summer of 2003, almost two years after that *soul-opening event* precipitated the transformative shifts that now impressed my world every day. I stepped into my new life with a bit of trepidation. It was like being at sea, not having ground beneath you to steady your course, while searching for a map to guide the way.

Sunay, my wise-beyond-his-years boyfriend, was standing in the doorway looking at me with disbelief. I finished speaking and slowly hung up the phone, "What?"

"You can't see what you are doing, can you?" Now it was my turn to be puzzled. "Something happens when you're around certain people – like you *need* them to tell you what to do. You're giving away your power, you know." I told him he was mistaken. After my recent divorce, I felt that I needed knowledgeable business advice in the many matters I now had to handle on my own. Sunay's silent look ran deep. He wanted the best for me, but I felt this was an unfair call, and decided to shelve it.

There was no precedence for how to integrate the phenomenal experiences that had rocked my world over the past year; a space had opened that revealed a timeless, formless depth of such riveting and wondrous magnitude that I knew I had been shown previews into the brilliance of our true potential. And while it was accelerating my awareness at warp speed, when lessons arrived to show the way, I often received them more begrudgingly than joyfully. At this point, the gut-wrenching lows were keeping pretty even with the spine-tingling highs.

Since I could find nothing chronicling this level of expanded consciousness, beyond books by deceased mystics and sages, which weren't that relatable to 21st-century life, the best thing I discovered to do was to just hang on tight, exactly as I did when I was a child sitting on the back of a fugitive horse. Rather than try to force the pony in any specific direction, which I was too afraid to do anyway, I gave him free rein, believing that he would ultimately head toward the security of *home* – and that's what I hoped for now.

With great determination I had put an offer on a new home

for myself. It was a complicated purchase; a commercial and residential building with many zoning issues that were over my head. But I had a vision of my new life, and when I walked into that spacious loft for the first time, I knew without a doubt it was exactly where I was supposed to be. I hired a well-respected attorney who specialized in commercial real estate, and began the process to procure this habitat for my new life. I didn't listen to the initial warning bells until I got a perfunctory call from the owner's attorney informing me that I was about to lose the property because certain essential documents hadn't been turned over. The clock was ticking, and my time was about to run out.

* * *

My next wakeup came in the form of my attorney's invoice. I was being charged, in the first month, *double* what I had been advised I would pay for his entire services. *Poor divorced woman doesn't know what she's doing*. Is that what he thought? Could I have drawn this event into my life from my beliefs that *I needed help*? Was I really so blind? Sunay's words were ringing in my ears.

I politely asked the attorney why my timelines were about to be missed. It was then he chose to tell me that after reviewing everything closely, his advice was not to buy. I was speechless. I needed to make sense out of the situation I was now in – especially since I had discovered this *undesirable* property now had three backup offers just waiting for me to drop out.

Important financial decisions were scary for me. My ex-husband was a business manager, and had always handled the money. I was in a new world, swimming in a sea of fear. I couldn't afford to make big mistakes. I'd hired this man to walk me through the rough terrain, to assist me in purchasing this safe haven, which would become my home. And now, through his brilliant counsel, I was in danger of losing it!? I felt so alone. Who could I turn to?

My inner knowing was about to teach me a big lesson. *Listen to the messages and trust.* I did when I found the property. I knew I was meant to live there, and I made an offer right away, no hesitation. Somehow, I'd gotten blindsided by this man's credentials. Thinking he knew more than I did, I handed him the reins, and true to form, he was trying to take me for a ride.

Each time I followed the guidance from my newly expanded awareness, the rewards were off the charts. I had discovered where to access the miraculous, the realm of the unpredictable, where the field of all potential opens. All that I needed to do now was continue listening and allowing it in. When I tried to fully map out my life as I had before, the synchronicity disappeared. I had learned long ago to envision and manifest my dreams, now I was learning to allow an even greater plan to unfold. The signals came in loud and clear – *trust*.

I got the message. I picked up the phone, called my attorney back, and fired him. Within 48 hours I became the happy owner of the building that everyone told me I shouldn't get. The coming years would tell the story of why this was the perfect decision to make.

* * *

Lessons to trust in the guidance from infinite intelligence, and to only take action from the inspiration given, continued to be played out against the backdrop of my new life. A medley of unconscious patterns became uncovered, showing me that, as strong as I seemed on the outside, I often took action from a place of fear. I didn't go to college, so when more *educated* people gave me advice, my first instinct was to deny my inherent knowing, and listen to the scholarly voices instead. Fear-mongers would appear as thoughts in my mind, celebrating the doubt they'd instilled, inviting me to walk away from the enlightened inner counsel I was receiving.

The building was high on the list of contention. The reality was, top professionals in their respective fields *were* telling me this building would not be easy to manage, that I could lose all the money I had, and to just let it go. Their arguments were valid. But the lesson was to *trust*. The handbook I had wanted was realized from a core of strength I didn't know I had, and it arrived like a gale force wind out of nowhere with enduring intensity.

Simultaneously, I learned how to quiet the apprehension that would surface like a nauseating vise-grip squeezing my insides. Sometimes I would take walks to release the anxiety from my body. I breathed in my connection with that loving, creative life force, and received the inspiration I needed time and again. I began to trust implicitly. I let go of my pictures of not being smart enough, of not being as educated as I needed to be, as my knowing far surpassed any formal study I ever could have taken.

* * *

In year two, another transcendent, indefinable, energetic experience skyrocketed my understanding into new stratospheres. It broke through even more layers of misbeliefs, that once this journey of evolving into higher consciousness begins, there might be only one or two defining moments – the threshold I found myself on demonstrated that the upgrades just keep coming. This one brought with it an unanticipated communication that this igniting power of peace was meant to be shared... and... by me.

This was definitely an unexpected message. I just couldn't imagine myself in the role of a teacher, and I was clueless of how it could happen. I needn't have worried; purely by giving agreement, I was shown. *Walk the journey, Marlise, learn to trust, learn to allow this illuminated stream of life's Energy to flow through you to each soul who is ready to do the same.*

The building once again rose to the occasion. Instead of being the final act of doom that would forever seal my fate, as had been predicted when the tenants left, I was inspired to open a studio where people who heard about the power of peace could discover what it would offer them in their lives. The magnificent walls, soaring 20 feet into the air, with windows overlooking the Pacific, became like arms of grace, encircling everyone who entered. This domain became a haven where many experienced the higher education they were seeking. And so it all began. It was a ride I'll never forget – the ups, the downs, the highs and the lows. It wasn't always easy, *but* it was always remarkable.

We act out different roles for each other so we can grow and discover whatever lessons are there for us to live in alignment with our true essence. If the building had been a character in a film, it would have won an Academy Award, it played its role so well. After three years I knew it was time to move. The developing neighborhood that originally looked like it would cause me catastrophic problems had become the *it* locale everyone wanted. The building more than doubled in value. When I sold it there were seven backup offers, each offering more than the last. People were mystified how something like this could happen. The simple answer is: trust. As the building transformed, brick by brick, so did I, through tears and laughter, as old ways of being were replaced by the luminous power that resides in every heart.

I could have stopped the process by resisting or trying to make sense out of the many difficult situations I found myself in, but why would I? Ultimately what I learned was to be witness to the miraculous unfolding of humanity's quest to know the Divine, the inner and outer universe we reside in. The act of trusting taught me the indefinable value of *trust*... for constructing my life in alignment with humanity's highest aspirations. Imagine that being the foundation for a future we all live in...

As you connect with the infinite intelligence that creates this world, you might believe that you will never have another negative thought... it isn't like that.

What happens is that you are now AWARE of limited thinking, of old patterns.

CHOOSE to rise above it. Consider where you need to do this now.

Each time you do this, life shifts, the road gets less bumpy.

And, you learn to TRUST that you are supremely guided.

THE BROKEN ZIPPER

My first day in a lodge in Kenya I was given a tent with a broken zipper. In Africa, this carries a whole new meaning. Monkeys love foraging goodies left vulnerable to their inquisitive nature, and I could hear them jumping on my roof, boldly declaring that a panoply of treasures was just within reach.

Sammy was sent to repair the problem before it really became one. He looked like an African ET with a gentle impish smile that warmed your heart the minute he beamed his sparkling white teeth in your direction. Within minutes of entering the tent, he felt the soundless tranquility that pervades the space where Stillness exists and asked politely about my line of work. After I told him, he asked to know this experience for himself. I sat with him in silence while the vibration of enduring peace ignited, and when his eyes opened, he had that inalienable sense of well-being radiating from his core.

I contemplated later who this person must be; this young African, who had grown up in dire poverty, been given an opportunity to learn English to get a job in a lodge, where one day a mystical collision of sorts would be orchestrated. Whether accidental or synchronistic, it was a convergence of the perfection of this grand adventure we call life, where each would afford the other a gift of magnified knowledge. The beauty and mystery of it all will forever astound me.

By the next day, my timorous friend possessed the quality of a fearless warrior. He reminded me of the undaunted, one-pointed seeker in ancient times, "I have to know more. Will you show me? Can I bring my best friends?"

* * *

The sky was dark from the rain clouds sending torrents of water shielding my tent from curious eyes. I had a momentary concern the lodge's cleaning crew might be missed from their duties. I felt sure their being in my tent was probably against some rule somewhere, and then I remembered – *I'm not in charge.*

Let the Universe take over, Marlise.
Okay.
No force can put asunder your time to know. This was their time. Whatever world they ventured to in Stillness claimed them to such a degree, they repeatedly couldn't hear my invitation to open their eyes when the session was over.
It's not over for them, Marlise.
Got it.
Their exhilaration spilled over into every area of their lives. They were the happiest cleaning crew you ever met! The word spread. Sammy and his friend Edward spoke to management about having a program for the lodge staff. They graciously suggested the room used for worship.

* * *

The solemn faces entering the *church* on that stormy night reflected the *curiosity* they felt. Many had been raised in religions brought to Africa from missionaries; others had indigenous beliefs. Their minister's first question was delivered with a passion usually reserved for the pulpit when denouncing life's temptations, "Where does this power come from? Is it Jesus?"

When you connect to the Stillness within, you're in the presence of infinite peace; it is the heritage of humankind whether your *preference* is Christian, Buddhist, Judaism, Hindu, Muslim, atheist, a spiritual path or a scientific one. Answering his inquest with the simple truth that The Simplicity of Stillness methodology is inclusive of *all* religions as it connects people to their hearts where there are no differences – clearly didn't given him the answer he was looking for.

The ardent clergyman stood up, and with a look of contempt,

walked out. The apprehension in the room intensified – and along with it the distrust. I had never experienced this level of unease. It was palpable.

When a common ground hasn't been established, when there isn't trust within yourself for discovery of any kind, even a simple request to close your eyes becomes a weighty proposition. These men had not been given many references to the meaning of the word *trust*. If I could give them some measure of confidence, just in me, then maybe they could find it within themselves as well. I wondered if Sammy and Edward's certainty had been shaken.

A large man with arms crossed in a manner that could be interpreted as either contentious or openly resistant began to speak. He questioned all that he'd heard. I later discovered that *Big George* was a respected and seasoned member of the staff, who many of the young men looked to for guidance. Working at a lodge meant leaving your home and family, often for months at a time. George apparently fathered their loneliness with a calming assurance that everything would eventually work out. I wasn't sure where George was going with this cross-examination when suddenly his booming voice exclaimed, "Ahhh! Now I understand!!!"

A big smile appeared on his face. His words were like a cool breeze calming the fires from having been baked in extreme temperatures. It felt like we had all been in a cooker; an evolutionary expedition. "You're not planning on leaving now are you?? We want another session!!!" It was almost 1am – *and*, it was their time. I joined them in a soliloquy of peace as the ever-present Energy conveyed through the recording emanated through the hallowed halls of this now-tranquil sanctuary. All questions had been subdued, at least for the night. Once the music stopped, everyone filed out and silently returned to their bunks. I couldn't wait to lay my head to rest. It had been a night like no other for this new teacher in a very foreign land...

* * *

The next morning informed me there were more lessons ahead. The minister and others had accused Edward and Sammy of bringing something evil to their lodge. I looked at their beautiful, kind-hearted faces and began to cry. I was so sad. Had I caused problems here? I began to question, to doubt. *I just want to serve. I feel so confused. Please help me understand. Show me what I am to learn.* A multitude of emotions crested over me like tumultuous waves at sea.

The rains poured down, echoing the desolation I felt, while tears streamed down my face. My usual optimism had left me, drifting down the flooded river now teeming with animals also lost in unknown territory. I knew there was another way to perceive this situation, the enlightened conversation was there in my head, but I didn't *feeeeel* wise or knowledgeable in this moment. Rahhhhh was a closer match to the pain that resounded from my aching heart and angry mind!!!

On the way to the lobby to check out, I heard that booming unforgettable voice in the distance, "Where have you been?? I have been looking for you all morning!!" *Oh no, all I need now is another confrontation.* But that was not meant to be. Instead, Big George's words echoed the pure delight he felt, "I want you to know we will have *all* the staff come to your next session!! I have been doing the Practices this morning and I will do them again this evening. I feel so much better!!"

The answers to my questions arrived with such speed that my spoiled-brat mind was spinning. I understood that whatever

Sammy and Edward were facing was brought to them as a gift as well. Maybe it was meant to strengthen them, to teach them about the trust we are all asked to imbibe.

* * *

When Sammy appeared at my tent for the last time to say his goodbyes I asked him why the minister was so angry. "Jesus taught that we all have Light within. Maybe I should have only told him that?" Sammy looked at me with such love, "When you go north from here and share this gift with others, they will be Muslim. You must tell them what you told us – it is the same for everyone. Keep your message as it is, Marlise."

Okay. I hear you.

Many had come forward to thank Sammy since our morning conversation; their foray into new territory resulted in peaceful hearts dissolving their stresses. With a hug and an irresistible smile illuminating his elfish ET face, Sammy returned to his daily duties, after telling me he would never, ever forget this time.

All that happened from a broken zipper. Some people might have thought that getting a cold tent with a damaged flap in rainy Africa might mean that nothing really goes right for them. And then... it might have turned out that way. And yet...

When you open to the light of the moon
You'll land among the stars
Amidst all those shimmering lights
It's then you'll know heaven

I will never forget your shining faces. I will never forget your love.

beyond your beliefs
or mine

is love

beyond cultural differences
love

not from the mind
not from the intellect

arising from the heart
the depths of pure grace

all else dissolves
all anger
all angst
all worry all fear

arising from within
beyond all words

love
love
love

THE GREATEST KNOWLEDGE

The question was burning a hole in his heart. All those years of study, all the passion, commitment, and love he had for being a healing professional – now felt completely meaningless. *When had it all changed?* Mark always wanted to be a doctor, but now he couldn't remember why, or even if he should continue. Every appointment mirrored empty faces having pointless conversations.

There were other distressing questions to be dealt with. One that he hadn't been able to articulate, not even to himself. Feeling unloved generates depression and suffering that materializes in every area of your life. It was appearing for Mark, around every shadowy corner. *Would it ever be different?*

Mark hadn't thought about it much, when he made the decision to attend an evening program, other than as an opportunity to spend some time with the friend who invited him. It was a special night in many regards; my birthday celebration had been planned for after the program. It was there I noticed his eyes, friendly and smiling – and yet so distant, as though deeply immersed in a *new world*. Mark said it had opened for him in the time of Stillness. Like a man who had just stepped onto the moon – a bit bewildered, not knowing what to do, he chose wisely to be silent, to understand more fully the magnitude of what he had been shown.

Ervin Laszlo, twice nominated for the Nobel Peace Prize, writes in *Science and the Reenchantment of the Cosmos*: 'Conscious experience is tantamount to looking at the world through five slits in the tower: the eye, the ear, the palate, the nose, and the surface of the skin. Yet this may not be the last word. Could it be possible to attain a broader view – to open the roof to the sky?'[1] When we are given glimpses into a deeper dimension, the kind that doesn't seem to be constructed by our intellect, and is key to unlocking more knowledge than we have been able to perceive, we sometimes shut it down, because it is so wildly unfamiliar. Mark had very possibly *opened that roof*, and needed time to assimilate the insights conferred to him.

If you can *be* with the awareness you are given and not undermine it with skepticism or try to make it less than it is, because it's unfamiliar territory, *the sky* will continue to part and allow passage. Several days later the aftereffects of the session were continuing to reveal new insights Mark described as 'extraordinary and life altering'. The questioning physician was still swimming in the lucid reality ignited from that special night.

* * *

Stumbling on his words like a runner who'd made a false start, Mark relayed the recent challenges he faced, "I'm not sure where to begin." He doubted why he had chosen a career in medicine, why he ever felt he could be of help to people – and that he was going through a *life crisis*, after the relationship with his partner had ended. The pain was driving him to question everything. The thoughts causing him the greatest distress were those that matter most to us all. *Will I ever know love? Will I ever be loved?*

The moment he felt the touch on his forehead as that lightning Energy force raced through his body in the time of Stillness, Mark's arm flew up as though pointing the way. What happened next was beyond his comprehension. "I was on a mountaintop in Peru. I wasn't having a vision. *I was there.* All around me were shamans and the archetypes in their world, like the crow and the jaguar." One shaman showed him a depth of knowledge he knew he had been taught before in other lifetimes. Seated around him, identifiable by their clothing, were indigenous healers from around the world.

"I started crying... I felt a profound connectedness to who I am, and the way I offer my services as a doctor. Suddenly there was a screen before my eyes, and on it a stream of faces were appearing and disappearing, one after another after another."

The images continued swirling by. All at once, Mark realized they were people he knew, people who had come into his life and *loved him*. He saw faces of people he recognized from his childhood, including friends that were in his life now. One face after another appeared, reminding him of how much he was loved. Tears streamed down and blurred the images as the block of pain in his heart began to melt. The stream turned into a flood, a serendipitous mixture of heartache and rapture.

"I just couldn't stop crying, because that feeling of *am I alone* completely dissolved. I was being shown all the love that has been given to me my entire life. And when the faces stopped, of all the people I knew, I began seeing faces of people I didn't know – and *I know I was being shown the future* – all the people who are coming into my life to love me, and those I will love." Every question Mark had was answered as the roof *to the sky* opened to give him a broader view – where he could allow love in and accept it as the gift of grace it was.

* * *

When we don't repress the knowledge that comes to us from the dimensions that exist beyond our everyday reality, we are able to perceive and integrate information in a new way. The messages Mark received not only confirmed that he was on the right path working as a doctor, it also offered him answers to the greatest knowledge we can ever have – the unequivocal knowing of how much we are all truly loved.

epilogue

A year after Mark had drawn this extraordinary experience into his life, he cycled through another round of relationship challenges that left him dispirited and broken-hearted. Each of us is different, and the journey we take to live consistently in connection with our essence is unique to our soul; some will take a long winding road, while others will have shorter distances to travel. And there will be many who don't even know the road exists.

While openings in the tower can bring to light solutions to our deepest concerns, the mind will take them, and the openings will close, if we don't continue the Practices that revealed them. Trust is essential – without it we can easily get stranded and *forget* the innate knowledge we've been given. Integrating this higher awareness into your everyday existence will bring a multitude of benefits streaming into your life.

It's not easy to watch yourself or the people you love take the bumpiest road, but with trust you will remember… that all roads eventually do lead home.

LIFE CAN BE BEAUTIFUL

Each day we have a choice… to spiral down with any activity that doesn't feel like it is going the way we planned… or to WITNESS the dance, to TRUST that we are guided, and become STILL.

When we choose to CONNECT with the infinite intelligence that brings inspired action...

Even in chaos, life can be beautiful...

And the answers will arrive... that evoke an even greater trust...

THE PRACTICE

LEARNING TO TRUST
our ability to trust surfaces through our connection
to the profound knowing within our soul

Trust is an ability to follow the intelligence of the heart over the mind, which is often dominated by societal patterns from our cultural as well as personal past. It is not about trusting any *one* or any *thing*; it's about placing your trust in the divine, by whatever name you choose to give it. In this chapter, 'Trials, Tribulations, and Other Bumps on the Road', people dealt with the challenges life presented them, and found solutions by assimilating trust into their lives.

Imagine that you have discovered the perfect vehicle to travel life's diverse highway – which you have – your own connection to the field of conscious awareness. You have the means of transport, now you want the best fuel possible. Trust powers your vehicle in the same way that the Energy of peace fuels Stillness; the end result is you needn't worry about ever getting stranded. This principle is often overlooked, and what it generates is beyond *trying* and *efforting*. Place your trust in whatever you believe created this intelligent universe and you will never be disappointed.

Guidance from the source of Truth will be easy to recognize, as it will always be aligned with the common principles of human existence: honesty, integrity, and love. What is possible beyond intellectual limited understanding only appears as you incorporate this principle experientially into your daily life. Similar to what happened when the people in this chapter faced adversity, and learned to trust their innate wisdom, you will also discover greater courage and strength to follow your convictions. Benefits that demonstrate extraordinary abilities and talents will appear that you weren't even aware you had. Doubt, cynicism, and uncertainty are replaced by an inner contentment that you are living in accordance with your highest aspirations.

Trust is not blind faith. You are only able to access this sacred attribute once you have connected to your essence. Instilled in this space of the heart is a deep knowing of why you can take that leap into unknown territory. It doesn't happen overnight, but once you see the many gifts that come your way by 'Learning to Trust', you'll feel comfortable walking a bit deeper into that limitless ocean each time you're invited.

Similar to the insight Sammy received – to trust in his experience and not reframe his speaking solely because some members of his community didn't understand his intentions. Even though he hit a few bumps along the way, what he received in his heart is the true gift that will give him courage to travel the many uncharted territories we all must face.

When you decide to embrace the new world that is opening for you, what is there will always be for your highest good.

Trust is the guiding principle that activates uncommon events beyond the scope of our imagination. You know you have incorporated this principle when synchronistic events become the norm. Once you have tapped into the Energy stream of life where infinite intelligence resides, and trust in the outcome, you travel each uncharted highway, allowing the unmapped and miraculous of life to appear again and again.

This Week's Practice:

- **Write in your journal** one thing that troubles you, and one thing you have always dreamed of doing, that you couldn't because of not having trust. It could be as simple as making a phone call to someone you didn't have the courage to contact, sending a letter you've always wanted to write, planning a trip you have been fearful of taking. Begin with something simple and allow it to grow.
- **Write down any insights** around your personal relationship with trust, and your intention to see it expand.
- **Listen to the Stillness Session audio**. Invite the quality of trust to permeate your heart and give you the courage to take action on the messages that arrive in the days ahead.
- **Write down one action step** you can take on the inspiration this practice offers, which can become clear in moments, hours, or days.

This is the road less traveled where contentment and adventure walk side by side. Now that you have the perfect mode of transportation, all you need to add is the *fuel* of Trust to empower your highest aspirations into the reality you live each day.

CHAPTER 7

THE DARKEST NIGHT
the night is always darkest before the dawn...

One day you wake up and find that your values are speaking more coherently than ever before. You no longer fit in the 'old' world you've left behind and the 'new' one is yet to fully open. It has become uncomfortable to even communicate in ways that aren't aligned with the person you're becoming. Your journey has taken you on an amazing ride; vast amounts of knowledge and experiential wisdom have enlightened your understanding. It's been a roller coaster of sorts, with breathtaking highs, as well as death-defying lows. You feel like you've made exceptional progress... until this moment.

The darkest night can propel you into a new level of consciousness, a shift in perspective that changes your life forever. It's nothing to fear, and is truly another gift along this winding road of higher learning. Become present to whatever you feel, whether it is anger, pain, sadness, shame, or feelings of unworthiness. The awareness it imparts is key to breaking through programming and beliefs that have denied admission to the miraculous of life. This process can give you access to a paradigm for living that is a veritable blueprint for the unimagined to exist in the now.

surrender
Walking the path seems so easy when it is laid out in front of you, synchronicities at every bend, a firm foundation beneath your feet. But what happens when that road starts to crumble?

All your hidden doubts, fears, and unhealed wounds are suddenly brought into the light of day. Those trapped emotions that have been quietly waiting for you to notice them are now demanding your full attention. *What is it you are being called to understand? Why is this happening?* It's called surrender... to no one other than your highest Truth, that limitless, infinite field of all knowing, regardless of the name you choose to give it. Feel free to replace the word Truth with any you personally use to describe the intelligence of this Universe, be it God, nature, or the quantum sea.

This is when you are given an opportunity to notice if your pride and ego have been trying to dictate the journey. These traits can't take you to the full measure of your dreams. The impulse that has awakened within is calling you to recognize the incalculable value of surrender to that timeless Energy of pure Love.

The *Mahabharata* is an epic tale of Indian Hindu culture that is filled with stories representing humanity's journey to know Truth. One heroic character that stands out is a woman by the name of Draupadi who was bold and courageous while overcoming adversity in her life. Duryodhana, on the other hand, was an arrogant, extremely proud king who decided to insult this exceptional woman publicly by stripping off her clothing in court. Draupadi thought she could resist with her own strength, but found it wasn't enough and became helpless as her sari began to be unwound from her body.[1]

It is at this pivotal point she recognizes that there is no one who can come to her rescue, except Krishna, representing the power of the absolute within, and so she releases the hold on her clothing. When Draupadi finally lets go and surrenders to the highest – in that very moment a miracle happens. The more her adversaries pull at the fabric, it keeps growing in length… there appears to be no end in sight to the sari she is wearing. When Draupadi surrendered to the limitless Love that is the Infinite, she was released from the bondage of her own slavery, the illusion of our separation from the divine.

the gift

People often speak of the dark night of the soul as a test. I have always felt tests were indicative of winning or losing. If we can see each difficulty that appears in our lives as a gift, then we will always receive the benefits, regardless of the momentary outcome. And, there really is no *final* outcome, it's just another marker along the way home.

Possibly because of the many fears I lived with, it took me years to surrender to that eternal presence, and once I did, so much of what I was afraid of – left me. The rewards are beyond your imagination: the Love you experience, the trust you gain, the courage you receive, the peace that floods your heart. You might think you don't have what it takes to get through it, but remember, you are never given anything you can't handle. Every step you have taken throughout your life has prepared you for this moment when you can leave the defensive, critical, reactive self behind and progressively move toward the considerate, generous, optimistic person you truly are.

signposts and treasures

The dark night of the soul is a signpost, one you will never forget. It is not a monthly or yearly experience. It is a rare event. And, there will be other *opportunities* with varying degrees of difficulty to learn about surrender. A favorite mythical tale of mine describes it so well, '*To defeat the darkness out there, you must first defeat the darkness inside'*. In this chapter is the story of a young man who faced his darkest fears, and also what took place in my life as we each passed through that maze of darkness and shadow.

At the end of the chapter are Practices that offer you the resolution and vision to continually move forward. When reflecting on this segment of the journey, remember what exists for everyone who crosses through this marker of transient anguish: you have the courage to confront any difficulties. You will find, as each person has who walked this tightrope throughout time, the emergence of treasures awaiting you... just on the other side...

THE ROAD TO HEAVEN
CAN TAKE YOU THROUGH HELL

The carpet reeked of old beer; the red wine stains were the kind that never come out. Sprawled like a child who screams in indignation at the loss of all that he holds dear, Jeffrey raged at his unsought and unforgiving plight. The worse part of it was, he knew he was to blame. *I want out. I don't want to do this anymore.* The tears burned as they rolled down his cheeks. He didn't wipe them away – maybe, just maybe acceptance of this agonizing pain could somehow be a form of retribution. Maybe it would serve as a penance that could help him get out of this god-awful, gut-wrenching hell he was in.

Feelings of utter hopelessness wracked his body as another round of tears fell on the grimy carpet. Partying, drinking, snorting endless rounds of his favorite nose candy. Not eating, not sleeping, hanging out with pseudo-friends, and working,

working, working. *Where did all the money go?* His internal cries of abandonment sounded more like the howls of an injured hyena who has relinquished all hope of ever being saved. A voice that mirrored his frailty responded, *You think you can't get out, because you're so deep in.*

The messages he had been ignoring from that knowing voice didn't stop. *Every dime you make is what pays for your partying.* It was true. Jeffrey worked two jobs and had nothing to show for it. *How did this happen to me?* His vehement cry echoed through the uncaring walls of his bare apartment, *I hate my life. I'm sick of doing cocaine. I need this to change…*

How could he be at this place in his life? He knew better. Jeffrey had studied psychology and theology, ancient scriptures and Stillness. He wasn't a *dumb-ass* – maybe a *smart-ass*, but he certainly wasn't dumb. How could he possibly have landed in this nowhere zone?

a step back in time…

Kathleen was a hard-working single mother who loved her son dearly. After graduating from high school Jeffrey felt he could now make it on his own. "Only I still need to live at home for a while. Okay?" It was then Kathleen inquired if I knew of a job for her son. It just so happened we needed someone to do Course transcriptions. The staff set him up in the office with headphones and a computer and gave him the go-ahead.

Jeffrey's tattooed arms and nose ring gave him the unmistakable look of many LA musicians, which we later found out he was. One day I happened to pass by the office door and noticed him peering into his computer screen as though lost in some other time where his mind had taken him.

The following week, Jeffrey introduced himself and told

me what had recently happened to crystallize the confusion he had been going through. He talked about the Energy he felt after listening to The SOS Course audio on that first day at work, and that it seemed to bring into awareness this enormous anger he didn't realize he had.

Jeffrey thought his mother was treating him unfairly, and decided he'd had enough. So *he told her off*, then he did the same with his girlfriend. When it didn't make him feel any better, he looked deeper. There were many things that troubled him, one being that he hadn't figured out what he wanted to do with his life. When he *got* that he wasn't upset with his mom – he took her to lunch and apologized. After that, he repaired the relationship with his girlfriend.

Jeffrey was enthused by the inspiration that was igniting his days with a new passion for life – that awakening power had lit a fire beneath him.. He told me I had really hit on something with this SOS method and that I should figure out a way for it to be taught in school, "This is the most important education you can get. I never learned anything in school that helped me see more clearly than this does."

In the following weeks, he would often stop by my office and share new insights. Jeffrey's journey of connecting to his infinite potential had moved into high gear. "I can't believe how energized I am. All the things that I've wanted to do and never had the energy for – I'm doing them now. It feels great!"

* * *

Life's dance of continual change took Jeffrey into new arenas. We'd see each other occasionally when he would take a course I was giving. I always loved spending time with him; 19 and yet ageless, he was bright, articulate, and filled with curiosity.

Whatever he communicated in programs would always be memorable, and would assist people of every age in their understanding of the adventure we'd all embarked on.

Months turned into years; I learned that Jeffrey had fallen in love and was living in New Mexico. He had made that big move out of his mom's house and into a whole new life. I would hear good news about him from time to time until the day when Kathleen called with concern – all communication had stopped.

About six months later, a beautiful card arrived thanking me for the blessing of bringing *Stillness teachings* into her son's life. Kathleen urged me to call Jeffrey to hear what had happened in that time of no communication. Since I was headed to New Mexico, I decided to catch up in person.

Jeffrey was in his element; the restaurant where he worked was beautiful, the food delicious, and his service fantastic. The hug he gave me lifted my feet right off the ground. The chef and staff had also found in Jeffrey the same loving guy I had gotten to know, only now he was a man. It was clear that a lot had transpired since we'd last seen each other.

* * *

The sun was shining; the music playing permeated the air between us with that unmistakable vibration of exquisite peace. Jeffrey's smile was that of a Cheshire cat who knows the simple joys of life. The road there had not been easy, it had taken him into the nucleus of hell itself. Jeffrey wasn't ashamed of it; he understood the experience got him to where he was in this moment. The night he hit bottom he learned what true surrender meant. Jeffrey told me it was the ultimate humbling experience, "I surrendered to all that I thought I knew, and then began retracing my steps, looking for guidance.

"I decided I had reached the end. No more cocaine. No more all-night partying. Something had to change. Then I remembered that you had gone through your share of drugs and had made it out." He recalled a Session when I spoke about the innate power we all have and how having a focused intention could set the stage for miraculous events. "And I remembered the peace I always felt in Stillness. And how much I needed to feel that again."

The next night Jeffrey was in a bar when a new friend sat down next to him. He let go of all pretenses, sharing from his heart why it was important to walk away from his current job, as it didn't surround him with the kind of people he wanted in his life. Most young men of his age don't often bare their souls, but his yearning for a new life now directed his mind and actions.

A week later, that same friend called to say she had just become the head chef in a top restaurant in the heart of the city, and wanted to know if he would like to join her. These moments of synchronicity are signposts that let us know we are back on track. Jeffrey's humility and act of surrender as he spoke out loud his intention to change called forward that organizing principle in the field of all potential to set the stage for the next step in his journey. It was a beginning, he could learn from the bottom up. No longer downtrodden the young man jumped at the chance.

Jeffrey had wanted to have a career that would align with the man he knew he was. In the months ahead, his spirits lifted, and a passion emerged to attend culinary school. How it would happen wasn't clear, and that was okay with him. He was happy, he was working hard, he was off drugs, he loved the people he worked with, and they loved him.

Our pilgrimage to the extraordinary has twists and turns. Sometimes it leads us through infernal regions we would never choose, and yet they are the determining factors in bringing the clarity of our purpose. I love that Jeffrey had the insight not to judge himself or be afraid of where the road would take him next. When the ultimate goal brings you rewards such as an ability to walk from your addictions and find alignment with your soul, it's worth whatever it took to land in that sublime knowing. The golden promise we have all longed to reclaim is not a distant dream. It could be a walk on the wild side, or a flash of insight, but surrendering to whatever it takes – is so healing that it breaks through to what is truly worthwhile.

DARKNESS IN BROAD DAYLIGHT

Unworthiness swirled through my stomach; the nauseous sensations that racked my body were holding me captive to a past I no longer wanted a part of. Memories appeared, leaving me in desolate gutters of my own making. How could I have done all the things I did? How could my life have taken me down so many dark alleys? *I'm a good person. I am. I did what I had to do – to survive, to earn a living, to get by.* Justifying the choices I made didn't help me feel any better. Instead, my mind continued its pattern of assault, searing images of life's early transgressions on my now fragile heart.

My thoughts journeyed back to when I left home at 16, and the feeling I had that I was in someone else's bad dream, that this couldn't be *my* life. I remembered the excruciating sadness I felt when I realized there was no one I could to turn to. I couldn't go home – I'd been disowned. I wasn't allowed to see my sister – I was *a bad influence*. I couldn't go back to school –

unless I lived with my parents, which for me, was impossible. I felt so alone. I was a kid. What was I supposed to do for work? I wasn't trained for anything; the only job I'd ever had was wrapping presents at Christmas.

A taste of forgotten agony resurfaced, fueling the sensations of distress coursing through my body. *How could my own father have called me a slut and a whore?* I hadn't even had sex at the time. *Why did he tell me I would end up selling my body on the street to support my drug habits?* When he would condemn me for what I hadn't done, it made me want to do it. I was already being blamed, so why not! I was hurt and I was mad!! I just wanted someone to love me.

* * *

My 19-year-old *knight in shining armor* had a hero's name he lived up to, at least initially. David was everything I ever dreamed of. He loved me with a passion, and there was nothing I craved more than that. David's rite of passage involved drugs from an early age; quite naturally I joined him on that joy ride into dangerous territory. He also happened to be a chemist who made organic mescaline from peyote, a psychedelic considered to be a very *holistic* drug. It gave people deeply religious experiences where they claimed to find God, or at least something close to that.

Since Native American Indians had used peyote in their traditional ceremonies for centuries, I figured it couldn't be all that bad. I found out it wasn't when the peyote seeped into my pores from the trashcan I stood in while grinding the earthen bulbs. Discovering hallucinogenic realms while being the chief assistant in the lab was definitely my kind of religion.

When I first became pregnant, we decided to get married

and soon after, David's drinking increased. My caring husband had become my father. He began abusing me verbally and then physically. When he took off six months after the baby was born, I could think of nothing else to do for a living except take over his *line of work*. The day he left, I became a drug dealer.

This was not the life I planned. *I was a nice girl.* But I needed the money to live and to take care of my baby. I sold the drugs to my friends because it was easy and I could do it without having to leave my child with someone while I went to work. Not too many mothers with babies went off to work in those days, so it never even occurred to me that I could. I fell into this new line of business never really thinking it was bad. I wasn't the dealer that movies depicted, who sold drugs to kids on the street. *I was the kid.*

* * *

And now on a misty morning in November of 2001, all I could think of was one event after the next where I'd fallen into that abysmal lonely life.

Drugs, sex with friends, then more sex, with lots of friends. Becoming a dancer at bars. Going on welfare. Doing even more drugs, living on Cuban coffee, cocaine and alcohol. Dating men I didn't like but was impressed with. Using sex as a way to feel powerful in a world where I always felt overpowered. Becoming a cocaine runner and dealer. Staying out all night drinking and doing coke, then drinking in the morning, and later, drinking and coking even more …

The visuals played across the screen of my mind. My heart felt like it was breaking as I watched one scene after another, feeling the shame that made me want to crawl in a hole and die. I cried out loud… at the futility of it all… I kept hearing in my mind the same paralyzing thoughts, 'I'll never be forgiven for all I've done. I'm not worthy, I'm just not worthy.' I was deeply ashamed. I saw the faces of people I'd been unkind to, and those who were unkind to me. I remembered all the sex I'd had without ever knowing tenderness and love. I recalled the many mornings waking up wondering just how much *fun* I'd actually had the night before.

What have I done? Who have I been? How could I think that I would ever know the Love and freedom I wanted, that I had been yearning for, asking for day after day? The inherent gift we've all been promised now seemed so far away. The tears continued to fall; the heartache and sense of hopelessness was overwhelming.

Suddenly, an *Energy* began to move through my body that was so powerful it was like a force of nature, like a storm that demolishes everything in its path, only it was demolishing my negativity by pulling it out of me. Then an amazing feeling enveloped my entire being, different than anything I'd experienced. The best description I can give you is that it was a sensation of *liquid love*, one that I never wanted to leave me. I wanted to stay in that exquisite vibration forever. There was so much of this Energy in my body, it was radiating out past my actual form. It was healing and so very loving.

I experienced absolute peace beyond anything I'd known. Light began streaming into the room and into me. I could feel it in my eyes – as though I had suddenly been given a pair of glasses that allowed me to see what I couldn't before. There was a luminous light surrounding everything. The sensations of Love streaming through my body felt like silken water, as though I was swimming in a shimmering iridescent sea.

In that moment, I knew I got everything I'd ever asked for.

This was not an extension of anything recognizable, albeit years of experiences spent in the company of masters of meditation and healers. I later came to realize this narrow beam, this crack in the void had appeared to illumine my past, present, and the possibility of my future – beginning with this occurrence often *called the dark night of the soul.*

* * *

Even though I'd been on a journey of discovery for more than 20 years, this experience was beyond what I ever thought possible – it belonged in ancient books of a mystic's past. How could it appear in my life, in the 21st century? To put it mildly, it rocked my world. My perception of life changed. I learned to surrender to the exquisite power of this Energy stream of consciousness, and as I did, I began to understand what was truly important to me and how I wanted to live my life. I was discovering it, not from an intellectual concept – but *experientially* as this form of silken Love streamed through my body, *and* empowered my thoughts and actions.

In the days ahead, feelings of powerlessness began to dissolve and were replaced with qualities of courage, sincerity, empathy, and enthusiasm. Fear and suffering began to lose its grip on me. And even though life's challenges didn't all disappear after that pivotal moment, as I integrated this awareness into each day, I could more fully accept life as it was, the ups with the downs.

* * *

I began to know Love, not through an intellectual understanding that can change in a moment; I *experienced* the *BE-ingness* of who we are that is loving, unchangeable, content, and compassionate. What I witnessed over time is how this Energy of peace shifted the trajectory of my life – and every person it touched, releasing levels of unconscious pain that has caused so much of humanity's suffering.

Not everyone will have to find this Love by going through the darkest night. Trust in the knowing if it does arrive, it will be at the perfect time and not before. What is most important to understand if you find that you are in the midst of this experience – don't push it away, as I did for such a long time. Surrender to it in whatever form it arrives. Discover what wants to become conscious. Know that you can make it to the other side. And if getting through this tumultuous occurrence can release you from lifetimes of pain, then isn't this exactly what you have asked for... the wonder of a realized and oh-so-very magical life...

SURRENDER TO THE KNOWING

Do you have a cave you go to... where you don't have to feel the challenges of the day... Does it keep you *safe* from noticing when you don't have the courage... to follow the messages you receive... that want to guide you into greater freedom...

If you only listen to your fears... you will never know the rainbow hues of Love's most delicious moments... that await you...

It's time to Surrender to that knowing now...

---------------------------------- THE PRACTICE ----------------------------------

SURRENDER
from the pain of suffering to self acceptance and peace
a healing process to establish the emergence of
true power...

When you are ready, or at the very least, when your soul is, you could meet with an occurrence often called *the dark night of the soul* that is similar to what is described in this chapter. This event occurs when we are ready to release habitual mindsets that cause our suffering. And while you might not *ask* for it, it is a momentous gift for the healing of emotional vulnerability and pain.

It is a one-time exploration that arrives unexpectedly, and its trajectory shifts you into an entirely different perception of your life. It can also happen with a diminished level of intensity at varying times along your soul's journey. Whenever it appears, remember the quality of *humility,* as it will greatly support this time of growth.

It could surface as an incredibly challenging time where everything appears lost, similar to what happened in this chapter for Jeffrey and for me. You are at a stage in your journey where you can't return to the way things were before, and you are not fully prepared to be where you want to go. As uncomfortable as this can feel, know that the conditions are perfectly set for a deeper truth to emerge. The best thing to do is:

surrender... fully... completely... and totally
Don't run away and don't make a plan. The best plan now

– is NO plan. Affirmations or any tools to gloss over these elemental moments of irreversible and incontrovertible insight and wisdom will not be helpful. Become still and walk the path that is being laid out for you.

Feel whatever wants to come up, whether it's sadness, hopelessness, confusion, doubt, or pain. Let the tears flow that can heal the beliefs that have locked away the full expression of your essence. Recognize the frailty of being human. On the flip side of this is your greatness, the Love at your core... For now, just allow yourself to be in the emotions rising, yielding to this ineffable time of recognition.

There is a common misperception in our culture that surrender is a place of weakness, but it's truly an act of strength. When you surrender fully, what you are doing is relinquishing the illusion of controlling what you actually don't *control* anyway. Simultaneously while surrendering, you are inviting universal consciousness, the part of you that exists beyond time and space, to take over and guide you. Most people spend their lives navigating the illusion of separation, living from the manipulation and control created by the ego. 'The Darkest Night', as daunting as it may seem, is a deeply healing and restorative process that releases these false beliefs.

When you are in the midst of this experience, grasping for anything that can soothe your soul, it's incredibly challenging to look at things from a higher perspective and to keep moving forward purposefully. One way to do this is to retrace your steps and see what you are meant to know; revisit memories that could assist you in discovering what you are meant to understand at this point in the journey. Actively communicating with and asking for support and guidance from higher intelligence will bring the answers. Whether you receive it in hours or days, you have opened space where greater awareness and new perspectives emerge.

The Practice of Surrender

- **Become present.** Breathe deep into an acceptance of all that surrounds you in your life.
- **With humility, surrender to the guidance offered.** Allow whatever you feel to gently wash over you, like waves of the sea arriving to meet the shore.
- **Listen to a Stillness Session CD.** With each breath, surrender into the arms of Love. Surrender into not having all the answers, inviting and allowing grace to enter your life fully and completely.
- **In your mind's eye,** revisit what brought you to this moment in time. Observe what you envision as someone watching a movie screen with silent images streaming by. Allow any fears or opinions to melt in a fire of humility.
- *Forgive yourself. Forgive others* and watch as even more suffering is released.
- **Invite greater awareness** to enlighten you with what you are meant to know, realizing it will arrive at the perfect time.
- **Write in your journal** whatever insights you receive, including being okay with not having answers now. Continue writing insights that arise in the coming week.
- **Embrace this moment** as the gift it is.

This Week's Practice:

- **Take a moment to acknowledge yourself.** It takes tremendous courage to face whatever keeps us in darkness. Remind yourself that whatever challenges you are dealing with in this moment, there is a greater purpose at play.

- **Know that this too shall pass.**
- **Follow the instructions of The Practice of Surrender.**
- **Feel yourself being completely supported** by the infinite power of peace in you.
- **Listen to the Stillness Session often** to assist you in moving through any challenging times similar to The Dark Night.

Remember, no matter how difficult things might appear, they are happening to align you with your own true nature. And, these times will pass. After all, the only constant is change. What was discovered, as seen through the eyes of both people in this chapter, brought about a release of incredible suffering. Like a caterpillar morphing into an exquisite butterfly... this is also your time, and it is a significant moment in the magnificent journey of your evolution.

CHAPTER 8

RETURNING WITH NEW KNOWLEDGE

when your capacity for love expands, it naturally flows out to all those waiting to know it for themselves

You have reached a point where you are often *in that flow of life* where synchronicity exists, where a commitment to your empowerment has revealed talents and abilities that surprise and delight you. An immeasurable *knowing* that is uniquely different than any formal education you've had inspires new choices and actions. This is a wonderful place to be, where you feel more love in your heart and you move through challenges with greater ease.

Unselfish love motivates your actions and elicits a new form of communication that leverages your mind to join in the celebration. New habits of well-being and balance have created a quality of life that, for the most part, transcend resistant patterns of the past. The welfare of others influences your capacity to believe in possibility and aligns with your newfound intentions and purpose.

effortless doing

Decisions are easier to make in all areas of your life, as you no longer fear that an *incorrect* choice could bring about some disastrous outcome. Doubt, anger, and confusion are simply muted images belonging to a person you no longer know. People elicit your support as you model the generous characteristics they aspire to. The energy you embody and your caring nature touches people deeply, even when you haven't spoken a word.

connecting with your innate genius
When you are *Be-ing*, you are connected to your innate genius, and are actually *doing* less than ever before. This is where you tap into that limitless field of potential that creates new pathways in the brain for *be-ing* in life, rather than *reacting* to every event that appears burdensome or demanding. You could be experiencing an *active* observing mode, watching how life moves forward without the usual *I'm the one who makes it happen* egocentric stance. This newly enlightened bond is fast becoming *your best friend*; issues and disputes are more rapidly resolved than the way any inflated identity might have handled them in the past.

You have gained access to the infinite mind, the living library of life. This is the *akashic field* that Ervin Laszlo writes about in his book, *Science and the Akashic Field* – where any thoughts that have ever been produced, can be accessed.[1] Imagine the possibilities…

integration and practice… or not
What do people do with all this conscious awareness? Integrate it. Bring it back into their lives and then share it with others. This is the wave of the future that has already begun, where each person consistently creates life from their highest potential. The more that people allow universal consciousness to flow through them, the more we will live by a new code of ethics where everyone relates to each other in a kinder, more loving, and altruistic manner.

You've probably heard the expression, *being kept in the dark*.

Well, this is the unfortunate reality of many people's lives, simply because they don't have access to the kind of information that can really make a difference. Theoretical knowledge without direct participation, in this instance, is of no value.

When you have access to limitless knowing, you experience a reverence and appreciation for humanity that becomes the grounding base of your existence. You can no longer take advantage of another without hurting yourself and actually endangering the benefits you are seeking. It also becomes impossible to knowingly cause pain to another human being. This is why a person who at one time might have been a bully or an abuser finds they now search out those who could fall prey to this kind of assault – and actually assists them in finding their own true voice.

pivotal moments of grace
Consider what happens in the lives of people who have had near-death experiences; they return with an enlightened knowledge that directs their actions in all future endeavors. It is reported that many find a deeper sense of purpose and appreciation in their overall lives. Pivotal moments like these, where windows open into that limitless dimension, are causing a shift in the world as we know it. And, you don't have to discover this knowledge solely through encounters with death. Thousands of people around the world have experienced this evolutionary threshold through a variety of awakening moments, and by simply listening to Stillness Sessions, and incorporating the conscious awareness streaming through them.

assimilation
It takes a bit of time to assimilate all these evolutionary shifts,

so it's a good idea to just slow everything down if you feel like too much information is coming at you. Inner calm and commitment to staying the path are qualities that will serve you well, so call on them anytime the remembrance of your journey begins to wane. If you find yourself back in confusion or doubt for any reason, revisit The Practices that support consistency. Every moment spent in this heightened vibration of peace will continue purifying what needs to be released and to impart clarity of what lies ahead.

As the Energy of infinite intelligence permeates and empowers your life, you naturally radiate Love into this world and the people you interact with daily. In this chapter are stories of people who took the knowledge they received into their own lives and back into their communities; The Practices they applied will guide your progress as well, as you become an even greater expression of the Love at your very core.

FROM POWERLESS TO POWERFUL
Katie and the Bullies

Big brown eyes, big black glasses framing them, a tiny heart-shaped face, and the sad countenance of one who has seen too much pain in a short-lived life. Katie said hello in a very grown-up manner, offering her hand in greeting, but without the usual smile you find when being introduced to someone for the first time. Her mother's entreaty to help her ten-year-old touched me deeply. The young girl's father had died suddenly of cancer, and the ravages of that malevolent disease had left his daughter and wife to confront a world without the security and love of the most important man in it.

Nancy was angry – and not only about losing the man she loved. Soon after his death she discovered they were bankrupt. With no money to even pay the doctor bills, they couldn't afford to stay in the dream home he had built for them. Nancy needed to get back into the work force, and she needed to deal with the outrage and sadness that now consumed her life. A well-meaning friend brought her to a Program, and for the first time in over a year, the anger that had frozen Nancy's loving nature began to thaw.

Katie's eyes reflected the emptiness she felt, the sadness that sent tears rolling down her face each morning, when that special someone wasn't there. Plain and simple – her father had *deserted* her and that's just the way it was. How could he have left her to fend for herself in a world where she faced ginormous decisions daily? How could he do that?? Where was that comforting shoulder to lean on, the dad who knew how to deal with life's uncertainty? She was isolating at school, her grades were dropping, and she didn't have and didn't want any friends.

* * *

We sat together on the floor. I asked her to breathe with me, to close her eyes and allow that soothing wave of deep peace to ignite within. The time in Stillness was brief. Five, six, seven minutes as that Energy stream of consciousness unlocked the gates where Katie had stored her broken heart, thinking it was in safekeeping. Once that sublime awareness penetrates the *prison walls*, healing begins. She spoke very matter-of-factly about how she could use what she had just experienced, "I can do this at school when I don't want to join in..." She continued, revealing the obscurity of her words, "Sometimes kids do things at school and everyone laughs... and I don't want to. If I do *this,* I won't have to join them."

Katie was talking about kids mocking and bullying each other. The peer pressure was evidently so intense that it was hard not to join in. Now she'd found the perfect tool to give her strength so she wouldn't have to participate. And so began the magical journey of a ten-year-old who clarified for all to see just how profoundly a child can assimilate their innate heritage and transform the world in which they live.

*   *   *

I didn't see Katie for over a year. She continued listening to Stillness Sessions, often two to three times a week before going to sleep. Life shifted for this shy, retiring young girl in ways that even her mother couldn't have foretold. Getting a role in the school play put her out in front despite her previous notions of wanting to hide, and she made new friends with a wide range of people, including the teachers who enjoyed hearing her unique perspective on life. From world events to everyday issues, this newly outspoken child always seemed to have something insightful to add.

The day began much like any other, but it was the day Katie would meet with providence in a crowded hallway at school. Susan was five-foot seven-inches tall, and while this height might offer incredible possibilities in future years, in third grade it often meant she was made fun of and humiliated. Today, that abuse escalated; a group of boys surrounded her, inflicting their schoolmate with the cruelest and most dehumanizing jokes they could think of. The head bully was taunting Susan with his cell phone, telling her how *utterly ridiculous* she looked, and how many people would laugh when he posted her photo on

Facebook. Backed into a corner feeling mortified, frightened, and helpless, with nowhere to turn, the young girl joined the many who hold these memories as indicators of their future. Only now, all Susan wanted to do was to make it go away: not only the bullies, but that demeaning feeling inside her – she just wanted to make it all go away.

Katie's inner strength had grown exponentially in the last months; acting from that principled quality of truth, she found herself walking directly into the circle of bullies. "Stop it! Just stop it!" she demanded. The lead bully shouted back. Katie struck at him, grabbed the girl, and took off for the principal's office. She'd had enough of his *meanness* – it just had to stop! Simple acts of courage can have a lifelong effect on many people's lives – this was one of them.

* * *

The principal immediately set a meeting with all the parents and teachers to discuss what could be done about bullying at the school and to implement their solutions. Bullying had become a crisis situation across the United States with many children taking their own lives – and this incident brought the problem to the forefront of his attention to finally be dealt with.

Parents of the victims of bullying often report that *no one ever stood up for their kid, that no child or teacher ever spoke up about the mistreatment of their son or daughter until it was too late, and they had taken their own life.* Katie's actions opened a new possibility – to be proactive, to look for solutions that could empower kids of what is inherently valuable in each of them.

What happened in the life of this little girl with big glasses that could possibly take her from being a shy, isolated child, to being a catalyst for change? She never thought of herself as a hero; she was just doing what came naturally. The trajectory of her behavior had shifted to match her *awakened* life. Her values altered her daily actions, and soon she searched out kids in the schoolyard who were misunderstood, the ones no one else liked. Katie said she knew they just hadn't found that love in their heart that she had – and she wanted to help.

* * *

The next year when Nancy decided to move, Katie's teachers pleaded to keep her at their school. They said Katie had become a role model for the other students. Always helping the least understood to be more self-assured, Katie taught them how to recognize their individuality, and find what was special and unique just about them.

People often think they'll be weakened by the innate power of love, and not have the strength to stand up for themselves or what they believe in. Just the opposite is true. Courage, commitment, caring, and engaging in life is what inspires Katie – and what she now teaches others is how to find that wisdom within themselves. This child who had been so afraid that she couldn't navigate life's uncertainty was now demonstrating, just by connecting to the source of her power, how we can all become illumined torches in each other's lives.

I imagine her dad smiling, watching the serendipitous consequences that occurred from his departure, and how they led his daughter to embrace the limitless strength and courage that exist in her today. That crystalline moment occurs when you finally understand, there is a perfection in all of life's dance.

Sometimes we think suffering is something we just grow out of as we mature. It isn't true. Awakening to greater consciousness is key – which can happen at any age. The road doesn't reach a final destination… it's a winding mystery that has healing occurrences at each bend of the road. When you can *see* it that way…

* Listen to a Stillness Session recording
* Allow guidance to unlock that knowing… of a fully empowered you

DROWNING IN DARK SEAS

"I hate my father, I hate my family, there's nothing in my life worth living for." Ana's jet-black hair hung down like a curtain shielding her from the world, her eyes barely visible through the dark glasses she wore. The lighting in the room was dim, and yet in comparison to her thoughts, it was a brightly lit space.

Ana was not someone who would have come to a Session to find a place of peace within herself – like most teens, Ana didn't have many references to that state of mind. The circumstances of her life had taught her what it was like to feel consistently judged, to not be enough, and to know the heartache and emptiness of not feeling loved.

After years of coping with severe migraine headaches and recently diagnosed with cervical cancer, Ana had reached the threshold of her pain. She stepped outside the boundaries of her beliefs the day she walked in the door of my offices. Ana's employer suggested she meet with me and find out for herself if this new Stillness *method* could help her to heal. This young woman's every thought and action resonated the anger she felt with the world, so much so she was generating even more of it – angry friends to agree with her, angry parents to blame, and an angry body that was voicing its pain so loudly, living with it was becoming unbearable.

She closed her eyes with trepidation to try out *this Stillness* even though in her words, she'd "... never been good at anything like that before." Almost immediately I noticed her body shift its rigid stance as that field of universal Energy filled the room, carried on the notes of the deep liquid music being played.

When her eyes opened wide with wonder, like a child who can't believe their good fortune on Christmas morning, Ana hesitantly shared the astonishing occurrences that had transpired. "The first thing I heard... was angry voices, so many angry voices... *and they were all coming from inside me.* And then everything turned to white light, this brilliant white light. And I don't know why, but I feel *so happy...*" There was a glimmer – you could even call it a luster – radiating from her face. Ana no longer had the lifeless look so often seen on those who are outraged with this world and their place in it. When I reached out to say goodbye, something inside me ignored her original *keep your distance* signals, and my arms wrapped around her like a mother embracing a lost child.

Ana held on to me as though I was the life vest that would save her from drowning in that dark sea she had been churning in for so long. In that timeless moment, I felt a tremendous outpouring of Love, as though the divine force resonating through this Universe wanted her to know unequivocally how much she was loved, and was utilizing my form to offer her this blessing. This stream of Love was flowing with such intensity Ana began to cry – and then to laugh, and laugh, and laugh.

What is possible as that timeless intelligence ignites is beyond conventional understanding. How can lifetimes of pain begin to shift in minutes? And not just *intellectually*, as nothing anyone could ever communicate could create that degree of transformation. Something out of the ordinary had occurred that would forever alter the life of this once troubled soul who had now lifted out of the sea of darkness that only an hour before shrouded her every move.

* * *

It was Valentine's, a special day that brought a lovely and astonishing gift to my door. Ana was not the same person who had entered my life just one week before; standing before me was a person who had completely erased the word *suicide* from her vocabulary. This was a woman who wanted to live. Her hair was styled so you could actually see her beautiful face. Her dark auburn eyes sparkled as she asked me with sincerity if she would feel today the same happiness she had felt at the last Session and if it would continue to stay with her, as it had most of the past week.

I trust that whatever we draw to us is always the next step in our evolution. I told Ana that some people feel a euphoric *high* for weeks and even months before it becomes incorporated into an elevated, more balanced vibration. It was also possible to have feelings of sadness, frustration, and confusion – *and* it would be just as beneficial, because it would ultimately provide her with a deeper truth of some pattern or belief she might not have been aware of. It was time to integrate whatever was coming her way by going deeper.

The depth of wisdom received from accessing this evolutionary awareness parallels what is written in ancient teachings by the world's greatest philosophers, poets, and sages. This is where the higher self intersects with pure grace. From here we discover the innate wisdom that informs us how we can participate in choreographing our future. Whether it's destiny or our soul's ultimate wish, events are set in motion that guide us to what is of foremost significance in the life of every human being – living in alignment with our very essence.

Ana wasn't angry about her painful childhood anymore. She got that it sent her in search of what she was discovering today, the greatest mysteries that have existed throughout time – which were bringing her more happiness than she'd ever known. This time when she closed her eyes it was with less trepidation. As she embarked into the dimension where true freedom exists, the boundless Energy of life danced through her. No need of swigging high-octane caffeine drinks, or stimulants of any kind. This is why, when the Session music stopped, Ana's implicit request was to always feel that dynamic happiness she was experiencing now.

In the weeks ahead, she learned how simple it is to not only find your way there, but how to integrate the serenity and empowerment so it alters the way you live your life every day. *Harmony* replaced the treachery of anger's insanity, *calm* replaced out-of-control, *sometimes* replaced never.

This became apparent when Ana announced, "Oh, I forgot to tell you! I decided to get my own place to live. I actually found the perfect place, and then I lost it to someone else. But it didn't bother me! I just know there's a better one waiting." Ana was living in a new reality, with a different way of speaking and thinking that didn't revolve around anger. She had a *knowing* of where to get that peace at her core. Ana knew that she was in charge of her life. If she didn't like it, there was no one to get upset with. She knew she was responsible for turning it around.

All blame dissolves in this paradigm of living. What is left is extraordinary. Forgiveness, compassion, empathy, and love now replaced the weighted anguish this once depressed teen had carried.

* * *

When Ana returned for her third and final Session, she spoke about her migraines disappearing and how she had thought she would have them forever, but now they were gone. And in a somewhat offhand manner, to let me know she was not surprised or impressed by it all, Ana said the doctors had no explanation to give as to how this could happen; they could only state their most recent findings – *her cancer had disappeared*. Just as surely as it had been there for so many months, now it was gone, not a trace left. She had returned to the hospital to begin a series of *special* treatments, and after only two visits, this almost incurable disease had left her completely. The doctors were dumbfounded.

How do you explain it? I don't even try. There are a few pioneering doctors like Andrew Weil, MD, *Spontaneous Healing*[1], and Dr Deepak Chopra, *Quantum Healing*[2], who speak about the various *miraculous remissions* they have seen or those being reported today – and what is possible when we integrate alternative understanding and medicine into the mix. I have learned to trust in the perfection of this journey and people's magnificence as it shines forth – and it does… it always does.

epilogue

In the coming years Ana stopped hanging out with angry friends and found new ones that made her laugh and enjoy life more. Her cancer didn't return, nor did her migraines. She recently wrote me a note about the many changes in her life and invited me to share it with you:

"I smoked heavily, drank to forget, ate to suppress, slept with an endless string of 'piss your parents off' kinda guys, and I covered myself in tattoos… addicted to this pain… I created illness in my body as a result. This was the wake-up call. When I was 18, I met Marlise. She gave me the tools that allow me to sit in Stillness… to truly discover what life is.

To think about where my life was 6 years ago, the anger that vibrated through me, the fear and negativity that I carried around with me, is almost unbearable. I am not a different person today, but an evolved person.

So many changes occurred over time that sometimes I didn't even notice until I sat down and reflected… the relationships that ended, the battles that went away, the reactions that ceased, the addictions that just didn't feel right anymore. Relationships that were simply choked by anger and negativity became light, and evolved into understanding and compassionate friendships. People around me truly reacted to my new energy. Instead of fighting for my opinion, I just speak the truth and let it be what it is…"

As Ana reconciled with her life and her parents, she became inspired to attend culinary school. In a few short years she had a catering company and worked for an array of celebrities. While Ana could be viewed as being at the top of her profession, she's decided to leave her job and travel, as her real interest has now become discovering how to pull more people out of the dark seas she once knew – and with the light she's become, I imagine she'll be the life vest that will bring many to shore. I leave you with her words of wisdom:

"This journey is not over… and it never will be… but my lesson thus far is that life is simply too beautiful to not let that laughter or those tears pour out of you… In this moment… just accept where you are and what you're feeling… and then move into the next beautiful moment… that's waiting for you… it's bound to get even better…"

AN INSTRUMENT OF PEACE

Be an instrument of absolute peace. Allow the power it offers you to be cause in the matter of transforming this world. When you choose not to live at the effect of life's challenges, you are being responsible for what you send out…

You can uplift, encourage and support more love to enter this world, through who you are BE-ing… and in every conversation you have…

Listen for limitation, and replace it with your love.

POWERFUL THINKING & SPEAKING
man has been endowed with reason, with the power to
create, so that he can add to what he's been given
~ Anton Chekhov

When we are overwhelmed or overcome by difficulties, we don't often remember the effective tools we have that can alter our circumstances the moment we put them into practice. Words are energy – what we think and speak influences us emotionally, physically, and vibrationally.[1] The Practice of Powerful Thinking & Speaking was developed to utilize what science and ancient traditions teach us about the thoughts and words we think and speak, and how these important tools used daily can create a future that brings significant value to each moment.

In this chapter, 'Returning with New Knowledge', Katie and Ana became conscious of their intrinsic power and the many talents they have. When we don't have this ability to 'see', our mind can become our greatest obstacle, as noted by Professor William Tiller in his book *Science and Human Transformation*, 'The soaring edifice of personal mind, so capable of touching all the glories of the universe, sees not glory when too rigidly constrained by old concepts and dogmas – then an unseen prison does the personal mind become.'[2]

The more they connected to higher consciousness, the illusion of their powerlessness dissolved and confidence in their abilities inspired them to share their gifts and knowledge with others. It happened simply – by thinking and communicating from the *knowing* that was now guiding their lives.

When you connect with that unwavering Energy of intelligence, your perception of yourself begins to change. A new set of beliefs eliminates your need for approval and acceptance and accelerates a natural healing process, giving you a greater recognition of your own self worth as well as your ability to contribute to others – just by BE-ing you.

Many thoughts that once influenced or dominated your mind are no longer a comfortable fit. Communicating in ways that are hurtful to you or another, begin to sound like the scraping of chalk on a blackboard. You might also begin noticing when you have thoughts that aren't projecting a favorable outcome such as; are you *totally devastated* – or *slightly disturbed*, do you have *horrendous problems* – or *are you dealing with a few challenges*, are they bad – or are they just *not conscious enough to be more thoughtful?*

repetition and pretension…

This is not about pretension or repeating words you don't believe – it's about creating a paradigm for life that empowers you. And it doesn't mean you *agree* with what is happening – you just learn to reframe it realizing that anything can bring you benefit – if you believe that it will. In *The Spontaneous Healing of Belief*, visionary author and scientist Gregg Braden writes, 'Belief is *our acceptance* of what we have witnessed, experienced, or know for ourselves'. He goes on to say, 'Our beliefs hold all of the power we need for all of the change we choose…'[3] Choosing an empowering vocabulary sets your heart/mind vision in motion, it is a conductor, entraining that magnetic energy field to respond; think it, speak it, believe it, see it – whether it's to the thoughts of a higher vibration or lower ones.

When challenges arise, there are always opportunities for growth – to see them as stepping stones to an extraordinary future – or as boulders blocking your path causing more pain and suffering. If you believe that circumstances and people can be the catalyst for old patterns or emotional pain to be healed, you will be one step ahead of the game. You can begin transforming any obstacles you see in your life, by becoming *aware* of what you think and speak. How you perceive what happens, makes all the difference in the quality of your life in each moment.

If you get caught up in the conversations in your head that depress you – then process what you *feel*; speak out what you need to express, even if it's only an inner dialogue at first. Then add new thoughts that lift you up – that are *hopeful, liberating, courageous, and caring*. The energy of these thoughts, and the inspiration they offer will energize a more resourceful frame of mind. As with all of The SOS Practices, when this process becomes a daily awareness and philosophy, every area of your life will magnify the benefits.

Once Katie and Ana were able to release the images they had of themselves as unworthy and unloved – which could also include any number of illusory and painful self-images carried from youth – they consciously began incorporating new and empowered beliefs of their true value. These beliefs reinforced their actions and soon they discovered they were communicating to themselves as well as to others – in ways that reflected confidence, love, and hopefulness. They became more courageous and compassionate, as well as creative and cooperative. As you begin integrating this Practice, you will be amazed at how quickly your life reflects the happiness you feel.

The Powerful Thinking & Speaking Practice

- **Become conscious, even rigorous** of the words you think and how you speak. Begin expressing yourself in ways that are aligned with your vision, and consistent with your intention of the future.
- **Shift gears** immediately when you hear yourself thinking or speaking in ways that are detrimental to who you are becoming. Change the sentence – even midstream – laugh, be flexible, have fun finding new conversations that empower your life.
- **Notice** if you have surrounded yourself with people who speak in a consistently depressing or unkind manner. **Give yourself permission** to love them – and move away from this vibration. Find people whose conversations uplift you.
- **Write your commitment** to think and speak powerfully – begin with a one-week vision. Then take it on week by week until you see the benefits reflected in what surrounds you.
- **Listen to a Stillness Session recording,** request to become more aware, and notice it happening each day.

This Week's Practice:

- **Write in your journal the words or thoughts** you think or speak often that do not inspire or uplift you. (You will be amazed at what you find.)
- **Listen to the Stillness Session CD**. Invite the quality of empowered thinking and speaking to enter your consciousness.
- **Write** in your journal the words or phrases you would like to use more. And which ones would you like to use less.
- **Write a commitment** to thinking and speaking in a way that inspires you to be the extraordinary person you truly are.

Watch how quickly signs appear that demonstrate the higher frequency of *matrika shakti* (word consciousness) and how it quickly it transforms your life. This week, continue writing in your journal whatever insights appear as you observe your thoughts and conversations becoming more uplifting. Anything is possible when we apply the inordinate gift this Energy field offers us through all our thoughts and words, moment by moment... in every day.

CHAPTER 9

SERVING & EMPOWERING OTHERS
from the loving example of one household,
a whole state becomes loving.
~ Confucius

When you have reached this point in your journey– as you look out on the horizon of the future, you will notice that challenges you faced along the way exponentially expanded empathy and compassion in your heart. One of your greatest desires now is to give back, to share the gifts and talents you've reclaimed. You aren't quite sure how to do this or what you'll be doing exactly, but you know that serving and empowering others is an essential element of expressing your true nature.

Knowing that our actions are an integral part of generating and unifying a world that values all of humankind resonates in the hearts of many people today. This is not about *fixing the downtrodden* as we have much to learn in the modern world from the many cultures who live simple lives with a truly dignified understanding of humanity's basic principles – the compassion, caring, and love for each other that has allowed them to thrive for eons. Every human being has something to offer that creates a wholeness, an entirety lacking nothing; we are a symphony where each instrument and note played is necessary to bring about the exalted music of the spirit.

the joys of sharing your gifts
What you find is that the more you serve and empower others, the more your life resonates with heartfelt moments, contentment,

and immeasurable appreciation. Being of service begins just by being thoughtful and loving in all your actions. You don't have to do something colossal. Consistently honoring and respecting yourself and others through your thoughts and actions are the small steps that will make a monumental difference in your life and the world as we know it.

riding the roller coaster

This Universe and everything in it is in a process of continual change; it can often feel like you are playing 'musical chairs' as the *enlightened you* trades places with the *unconscious you*. It gets easier and more effortless to stay *seated* in our loving nature as we evolve. Accepting this with a willingness to progressively develop is an essential element for managing tough terrain. And, people often tell me at this stage that the lows don't affect them nearly as much as they did before.

It's great knowing you have the tools to decipher life's varied circumstances. Everything you have discovered, even when dropped to your knees in humility, could be the very thing you offer back to the world to improve the lives of others.

you can't give what you don't have

We all know what it's like to be hurt, lied to, taken advantage of, and mistreated. With all the potential risks that come from exposing our vulnerability, what is it that actually moves human beings to be willing to open their hearts to the wonders of Love? The answer: *experiencing infinite Love* fills the well to overflowing, and teaches you about life in a way nothing else can.

I am not talking about societal concepts of romantic love that include a checklist of preconditions that need fulfilling.

The Love that I am speaking of is what you connect with when you're allowing that dynamic, immeasurable life stream to flow through you. This Love is present in every cell of your being, regardless of whether you know it or not; it is the matrix of all of creation. This is the Love that poet saints in bygone eras attempted to express as they wrote through the joyous tears of their experience. It is not so distant anymore. When you experience and embrace it, you'll discover you have a limitless supply to share with others.

the ripple effect

Like the ripples of a pebble tossed in a lake, as the waves grow to include the entirety of the sea – you learn to appreciate the goodness that exists within you first, then your family, friends, and associates. Before long, that understanding has grown to include the global community as an intrinsic part of your experience. We are all threads in a wondrous cloth woven to wrap the world in a blanket of indefinably powerful Love.

The Energy of absolute peace breaks down the barriers that have made us feel separate from each other and God, by whatever name you give that universal principle. Once your heart opens to the breathtaking spaciousness inside, you will never want it to close again. As this magnifying presence expands, your inspiration, of how to pave the way for others to recognize these gifts of the heart for themselves, will grow.

the exquisite gift of universal love

Over the last years I have observed this stream of peace alter the very fabric of people's lives creating a ripple effect inspiring others. Some of their stories are contained in this chapter, 'Serving & Empowering Others'. There are many people around the globe living by these principles today, it's just what happens when you experience the deepest dimension of who you truly are. The SOS Practice at the end of this chapter was designed to support this powerful magnification in your life as well. Enjoy watching the ripples you send out as they merge into a sea of encouragement, understanding, and Love... for all.

ANCIENT CULTURES, SIMPLE TRUTHS
Two Hands Wash Each Other Clean

I first heard about the Dogon when reading a script for a film that was somewhat like *Indiana Jones* – filled with adventure, mystery, and archaeological digs. This ancient tribe had knowledge about the stars and the cosmos even before telescopes were made that could reference the planets they spoke of. Living in red hewn cliffs overlooking endless desert rock and sand, these primitive people seemed to have knowledge that is still unexplainable today. How could you not be intrigued? Well, I certainly was. And years later, the possibility of traveling to these far-off lands became realized, spurred by messages from within, telling me that Mali, Africa, was exactly where I was meant to go.

From the beginning of time, the Dogon kept their knowledge intact by passing it down from one generation to the next in the form of storytelling. Nothing was written down. They were a mysterious people, and in this time of my life, when so much of what I discovered was melting the impenetrable beliefs that had guided my previous existence, it was time to look deeper. If I could learn without old concepts of the past playing in the tape recorder of my mind, how much more could I become conscious of that would enlighten my life?

It wasn't long before those doors opened, and the way appeared. It was time to go.

* * *

Hogons, the spiritual leaders, are said to have special wisdom passed down to them through their ancestors. When Mikaelu, our Dogon guide, spoke of the spiritual head of Sanga, it was with the utmost respect. Standing in the doorway of his unique mud home, singular even for Mali, with columns that store ritual trinkets, the 97-year-old man appeared disinterested when the translator invited him to come out and speak with us. From the looks on the faces of people standing nearby, they also had no luck. Reluctantly, they walked away.

The Hogon's reaction is not surprising. The local guide repeats Mikaelu's sentiments that it is not customary for these revered men to visit with anyone who is not a member of their tribe. And yet, I feel that something is about to happen. It's not time to go. I ask Mikaelu to let the man know that I have come to ask for his blessings with great respect. The Hogon sits quietly, surveying all that is happening on this day that will bring the uncommon into a new reality for all who stand at the gate – those before it, as well as those behind.

Suddenly, he nods. He will meet with me at the Toguna, the high council of meeting places where only truth must be spoken. He is on the move now and things begin happening very quickly, almost faster than time allows for the village guide to close his gaping mouth.

A face-to-face with a Hogon is a great honor, and to convene with him at the Toguna is very special indeed. When you enter the *stream of life* that exists for us all, you do not have time to evaluate what happens, as that would place you on the shore. Instead, you learn to just *be,* without expectations, so everything that occurs can capture you wholly.

We all want to live in this state of eloquent alignment more often than not. Even winning Olympians find these heightened moments dissipate once they have left the field of their endeavor. That's why integrating the experiential wisdom revealed in Stillness is an essential element to maintaining our connection, and it is tantamount to having that *gold* streaming through every area of life. This is about choosing to know more deeply how to interact with what informs our very essence. Today, this immeasurable field of knowing would offer me higher planes of education – considerably widening the lens of my understanding.

* * *

The Toguna's purpose unraveled for me some of the mystery of how these indigenous people maintained peaceful relationships within their communities down through the ages, without any law enforcement or jails to safeguard them from the evils people have wrought upon each other throughout history.

Within the framework of this space, all disputes are handled. Children are invited to attend, so they can learn how to settle differences while still respecting the other person. Everyone is honor-bound to speak the truth and to follow through with the elders' decision. Once made, it is in the hopes that the grievance will soon be forgotten and left in the past. This method of jurisdiction is astoundingly elemental and it has been serving the Dogon for as long as they can remember.

How is it that the most elemental practices can offer us the most insightful truths? We have much to learn from the people of this world who live such simple lives.

The Hogon seated himself where the Toguna crowned him like a resplendent portrait. It was a beautiful sight. The many hues of Sanga – the taupes and creams of rocks and stones coalesced with the shades of muted espresso on the face of its transcendent commander. The colors blended with their surroundings, allowing a harmonious merging of man with the elements.

Brandishing the scepter of all Dogon spiritual leaders, the Hogon graciously welcomed me. I extended him my appreciation not only for his vast knowledge but also his servitude. "Your people have a great understanding for living connected to this Universe, and so peacefully with each other." From English to French to the local dialect, our communication could have created challenges in being understood. But what we express through the energy of our being is always heard louder than any spoken words, and what we send out instills fear and doubt or the opposite – trust, which is what resonated between us now.

There was an ease in our conversation and it seemed to grow incrementally with each passing moment. I asked if it was possible to receive blessings from this man who knew how to counsel his community so wisely, as I also wished to be of service. When he inquired what I did I told him how I'd been traveling the world teaching people how to ignite this infinite Energy within, and how it had helped many to find peace in their hearts. The venerated leader nodded, "The work you do is very, very good. I am happy to exchange my knowledge with yours."

I thought his kindly response had meant that our time had

come to an end... until I heard, "Will you give it?" When I didn't respond, the translator repeated his words again but this time with gentle insistence, "He wants you to make Stillness... *now.*" My mind was trying to absorb the moment, when I heard myself whisper... *ohhh... now...*

In the middle of the village square, with the sounds of children playing in the distance, I closed my eyes and opened my hands. It was one of those timeless moments when the world becomes completely still. No music was needed; the gentle wind swept around us becoming the *dulce melos,* that sweet melody of the ages, allowing the gentleness of transcendent peace to be felt.

The Hogon's eyes closed, the guides instinctively opened their palms, minutes dissolved into the golden euphony that only pure presence expresses. A honeyed calm spread across his face. When the ancient one opened his eyes, they told the story of what had transpired, while his words conveyed the depth of wisdom arising from his heart. He spoke of his wish that there be more peace in the world and that by *bringing our knowledge and prayers together, it would '... make one big knowledge to be even higher', and that it would have a lasting benefit.*

Once trust and respect is established, the gates that are locked fly open. How often do we hear people stereotype and dismiss another human being with words of bias that cross every culture we don't understand. Such as I had heard before leaving on this trip: "Poor Africans, what could they possibly have to teach us in the modern world?" And yet, the wisdom this spiritual leader and his community have to share could change the face of how nations and people treat each other in centuries to come.

The teachings continued to pour forth, "What can one hand

do? With only one hand you are limited. *But two hands can wash each other to become clean.*"

Our prayers for each other and the world were like those hands. When we come together, what we can accomplish is of greater value than what we can do on our own. *With only one hand you are limited, but two hands wash each other to become clean.* What an exquisitely simple and profound truth.

The divine principle that guides each step of our journey had sent a magnificent messenger to provide these truisms of ancient teachings. As I leave my new friends, immense appreciation engulfs my heart and mind. *Thank you for the wisdom that prevails over ignorance and prejudice, and for bringing this heartfelt knowledge into our lives that invites love to conquer all.*

All we need to know lies within us, and all we have to do to uncover it – is ask for our deepest knowing to guide the way.

MYSTICAL, MYTHICAL, MODERN GODDESSES

Lizzy could have played the heroine in her own life story. She *loved* the adventures of gods, goddesses, heroes, and heroines in Greek mythology; those enthralling myths that likewise contain the origins of human woes. Although she dreamed of heroism, when we first met she was infinitely more inclined to express the latter. How we met was a mythical tale in itself. It was autumn in Sedona, the air was cool, and some of the trees had turned a golden hue, which made them stand out even more against the magnificent red rock cliffs. I was enjoying some reflective time when I received an unusual call.

"You're not going to believe this!" Francis, a dear friend who also happened to be my real estate broker, was laughing, enjoying the mystery of what she was about to share, "Someone wants to buy *the building*!"

"But it's not for sale. How did they find it?"

"It's a unique property, Marlise. Why not just let them look?" She was speaking of a space I was inspired to buy when beginning my *new* life – *The Building*, which unraveled its own mysteries in Chapter Six.

As unexpected as that call was, the one I got two days later was even more unconventional. "We met with the buyer… and, well… his wife wants to meet you and have a Private Session." I was learning to live on the edge of surprise, as nothing about my life was *normal* anymore, but this series of events was definitely adding to my wonderment.

Intrigue collided with tranquility when I received the third call: the buyer's wife *happened to be* in Sedona and was hoping to meet me – tomorrow! How often does someone appear in your life – to buy your home when it's not on the market, go out to dinner with your broker, and discover that their spouse is staying at the same hotel you are – in a different city and state?? I mean really, what are the chances?

* * *

It was an incandescent night, the moon was almost full and a fire was blazing, sending its warmth into a room that was soon to become even hotter. Ancient texts tell us about the inner fire initiated through awakening Energy – and how it burns away the pain of lifetimes that reside in the energetic field of the body, continuing its journey of purification until we are reunited with truth.[1] Lizzy and her sister, Isabel, ventured into this province that destiny delivered to their door, respectively with excitement and trepidation.

While they had the same mother whose disturbed mental health had put deep-seated hurts in motion, they each dealt with their past in a uniquely different manner. Lizzy was a hip, 30-something wife and never-want-to-be mother whose heartache from the past ran too deep to even consider the possibility. Nerves, depression, hearing loss, and a multitude of female problems resulted in Lizzie taking a plethora of prescribed medications daily. Angry about the childhood she felt had created these illnesses, Lizzy was no longer speaking with her mother, and planned on keeping it that way.

There was distance between the sisters as well, and it was more than the geographic mileage between LA and New York. Isabel was a 20-something sex-and-the-city woman, earning a good living as an editor in an established publishing house. Her big sister often gave suggestions on how to live her life. They were not well taken. After all, they came from a woman who was submerged in a world of mystical gods, and Isabel had been living by the practical laws of survival for years. This trip to Sedona was another of Lizzy's attempts to shrink the ever-widening gap between them.

Isabel's health was as challenging as her sister's: lengthy bouts of depression followed each love relationship that ended badly, which was a frequent occurrence these days. Her greatest fear was that she might become schizophrenic like her mother and she had begun to consider suicide as a way out. Neither could ever have imagined the healing journey that would begin on that night, for these sisters whose hearts were so entwined, and in such pain... maybe only the gods.

* * *

Watching people shed layers of grief and suffering is what that fire of invincible Energy initiates. Whenever I saw Lizzy another blanket of pain had come off. She got entangled from time to time and would forget to recognize the woman emerging from that multilayered cocoon. Then she'd remember to get back to the Practices that calmed and inspired her. Her letters described what it was like to release those layers that had held her captive for so long: 'I had an amazing paradigm shift yesterday – a moment of self-acceptance. It was powerful and wonderful... I have begun to believe in myself and what I deserve.'

Lizzy became inspired to focus on her dream of being a singer, even though she was partially deaf in one ear. She wrote songs that were so moving they could light up the path of anyone walking the dark roads she once traveled. The multicolor pills that had been her daily breakfast dwindled to almost none. An enthusiasm for life replaced her anxiety and she returned to college to get a Masters degree, writing a thesis on her beloved mythological heroes and heroines that reflected her solitary journey out of the *pathos* and into the *logos*. The harsh reality she had dealt with for years diminished to the point of nonexistence.

* * *

Isabel was also on the mend, even though her journey ventured through more dark nights. Whose idea is it anyway, that once we *awaken* we will never have another bad day? These concepts are the invisible beliefs that keep happiness away from us. Any time the light began to dim, all that Isabel needed was a reminder of who she was beyond the drama her mind played like a first-run movie, and she'd allow the infinite dance of Stillness to melt her into the tranquility she found there. Before long this oh-so-cool lady began sharing oh-so-much love with her friends, many who still walked in the shadows she once called home.

More astonishing events occurred: Lizzy embraced the future she hadn't wanted – that of being a mother. 'The block I had was that I believed my life would end when my child's life started.' She agreed to meet with her mother and together they began healing their wounds from the past.

The prospects of an unimaginable future didn't stop mounting. This woman whose female anatomy was *so screwed up, she'd never be able to have a baby* – got pregnant! The love that began to fill her world was so huge she needed an outlet to share it. When she found *by chance* a school in need of teachers – even more than the donation she was calling to offer them – inspiration struck, and Lizzy's journey took a new turn. She knew exactly what she was meant to do.

* * *

They stared at her with eyes that have known too much heartache, too many lies, and too much pain to even want to live. Some had been raped by family members – fathers, uncles, cousins, and *friends* who had never shown them any respect, or given them any reason to respect themselves. It made her want to weep. All the pain of her childhood came racing back, but now it came to aid her, so she could share with these girls, some as young as 12, that she had also made it through the darkest of times.

She gave them love and it melted their core, and then she gave them even more. Lizzy shared her own suffering. She sang her songs to them, and slowly their hearts opened. Their damaged hearts found the tender goddess within. They learned to forgive and offer love to their unborn babies. Myths became reality as the power and peace Lizzy had found spread to the next generation so they could also become the heroines of their story.

epilogue

Often people feel that hurts from the past can never be healed. From, *I never want to see my mother again*, to creating a loving relationship with her was something Lizzie never bargained for. Not that they became a *model* family, but one that is a work in progress, which is authentic, and leaves space for growth and an expansion of caring and kindness. Lizzy's letters represented the challenges as well as the hilarity of the process, as the new grandmother became an integral part of family functions and travels.

And, oh, by the way, I don't believe Lizzie and her husband were ever meant to buy my house, it was just about destiny and how the Universe brings people together when it is meant to be... that exquisite dance of the soul to know its very self and to share that brilliance with others.

When that bell of awakening rings within... it doesn't only go off one time and you are done... the journey continues... and each time you see another block in the road, where anger, resentment, or resignation exists... there is an opportunity to go deeper.

- Dive back into The Practices
- Feel the enormous release that connection to absolute peace offers...
- And then share your enlightened life with everyone you possibly can...

HEART TO HEART

We are meant to play this *game* in a way where we enhance each other's lives... And the more we recognize the opportunity each person presents us with... the more we connect in heart-to-heart communication... Doors open, possibility abounds.

Appreciation and caring are the common denominators of each interaction.

Aaahhh Life... Thank you... Thank you...

and Thank you once again...

--- THE PRACTICE ---

APPRECIATION & BEING OF SERVICE
I now understand that my welfare is only possible if I acknowledge my unity with all the people of the world without exception.
~ Leo Tolstoy

Think of how you feel when you are appreciating anything – life, your family, your friends, or the beauty of this earth. That energetic vibration of appreciation is like a soothing balm to the soul. Not only does it *feel* good, the resonance of this magnetic field can cause shifts in lower emotional states of frustration, resentment, and injustice. Consider what happens when you are upset and your child, friend, or spouse tells you how much they appreciate you. If it's only lip service, it won't be effective, but if they are magnifying an expression of Love from the heart it will begin to melt whatever anxiety you feel.

'*Be the change*' is a meaningful phrase we've heard over and again, but how can we consciously apply it to our own lives? When we recognize the impact we have, purely by being responsible for our state of mind – and how that affects the electromagnetic field that surrounds us, we realize that every moment sets in motion an incremental modification of such import that its trajectory could create a global shift in consciousness. How can you participate? A deeper dimension opens in your own life as you recognize the significance of your role in creating a peaceful, sustainable future for this world, solely by living in connection to the Energy stream of peace in you.

When you become *still*, you can tap into a level of presence where your fears, doubts, and resentments begin to subside; where that Energy of equanimity magnifies an expression of thankfulness. This simple Practice where you focus on appreciation, can incrementally increase your overall enjoyment of life.

being of service is a natural evolution
for becoming a more loving and caring society

This life force Energy that opens the heart and inspires you to share the innate wisdom, love, and clarity found there – is what will ignite an evolutionary shift to become a society that lives in harmony with nature and each other. In this chapter, 'Serving & Empowering Others', each person found that their experience of appreciation grew to where they literally began searching for ways to contribute to people's lives. As in the case of Lizzy, where she discovered that her own gifts could make an immeasurable difference to the young girls she taught – while Isabel found others in depressed situations, similar to what she had known, and now could invite them to find new pathways out of their own darkness.

In many people's stories throughout the book, the theme of service is quite naturally replicated; The Angry Man instantly wanted to share what he had found with his entire community, Katie gave back by searching out the kids who were vulnerable to being bullied at school, Jake made films that inspired compassion. When your life resonates with heartfelt moments and immeasurable blessings, you just naturally want to give back. Being of service is a key practice for living with expansive Love in your life and for fostering this experience to grow in the world.

* * *

As this higher vibration of appreciation and well-being expands, you gain access to the invaluable qualities of well-being, vitality, and resourcefulness, and yes, even more synchronicity. Adding time spent in appreciation as a daily or weekly practice, you will discover the journey ahead filled with promise and the singular adventures that make life so worthwhile.

The Practice of Appreciation & Being of Service:
- **Write in your journal** a list of the things you appreciate in your life. Write anything that comes to mind, no matter how big or small. Notice how it makes you feel. On one day, you might focus on your family, another on your friends, self, nature, world, work, and home. It's a great reminder of the many blessings that are in your life.

- **Contemplate** how you can be of service. **Write down** whatever comes up.
- **Listen to the Stillness Session CD.** Whether it is a *walking Stillness session* or one where you have found a quiet place just to lie down and fully relax.
- **Reflect** on people you've met along life's journey and what they have taught and offered you along the way. Allow your heart to fill with gratitude.
- **Write down** any ideas or inspiration you have.
- **Share your appreciation.** Find opportunities to extend appreciation to others through your thoughts, words, and actions, and observe your life transforming as well as the lives of all you touch and serve.

Writing down what you appreciate is very powerful – it tends to take your focus off what pains you and puts into action what makes you feel good, thereby shifting your focus off any negative chatter that could be present and moving into a more resourceful vibration. It's not about painting a happy face on storm clouds, and it is about disciplining the mind. Here are a few simple suggestions for moving from upset to appreciation:

- I love the beauty of nature. (Just be with this thought... how does it feel...)
- I appreciate how kind people are to me. (See the faces of people who are supportive and loving in your life.)
- My life (on the whole) is very blessed.
- Even the most challenging times have brought gifts of knowledge into my life.
- Somehow I seem to make it through all of life's difficulties and I find that (eventually...) everything works out just fine.

(Notice if you are feeling better – add new thoughts that continue bringing the feelings of appreciation higher.)

This Week's Practice:

- **Contemplate** the people you appreciate and why. **Write a list** of the people that have touched and inspired your life.
- **Write in your journal** different ways to express your appreciation from a simple thank you to an acknowledgment of who they are, or of work they have done.
- **Reflect** on different ways you would like to be of service to others.
- **Take a Stillness Walking Session** and as that clarity and inspiration arises:
- **Take Action** and make a call, send a note, or email and just communicate your appreciation. Make an appointment with the person or company you want to offer your services to and let them know how you feel. Make being of service and appreciation a daily habit.

This is the gift that keeps on giving; each word or thought of appreciation or service you offer comes back tenfold. Consider how very simply this can happen: through a smile, or an act of kindness. Realize that you are enriching not only one person's life, but many – as that Energy of peace magnifies exponentially, it transforms your life, and evolves consciousness throughout the world.

Your experience of the world will be profoundly enhanced, by turning your attention toward the true reverence of life... appreciation. What an extraordinarily transformative and yet simple way to make a difference... every day.

5

WHERE DO WE GO
FROM HERE?

CONSCIOUS LIVING
Fulfillment, Freedom & Peace

When you experience your innate heritage and live from a loving, empathic, inspired heart and mind – your life transforms. Simple moments of profound heartfelt connection dramatically elevate your perception of what is possible; you become filled with an enthusiasm for sharing this infinitely freeing wisdom with others.

Embracing the conscious awareness being expressed through you redefines your life trajectory and supports a global community where the Energy of infinite peace is woven into every area of life, bringing fulfillment, freedom and peace.

WHERE DO WE GO FROM HERE

Man didn't believe he could fly – until the day he did. The four-minute mile was said to be impossible – until it wasn't. Many thought it inconceivable to educate a blind/deaf person – until the day a determined teacher broke through her willing student's isolation. Wilbur and Orville Wright, Roger Bannister,[1] and Anne Sullivan[2] weren't heroes, they were ordinary men and women who dared to envision and act on an idea that was meaningful to them.

The coherent power of my heart/mind intention with what I *believed* was possible resulted in a sequence of expanded reality experiences, which in turn offered me a new lens through which to view all of life. The events I witnessed as this life force Energy ignited in people around the world dramatically changed my understanding of what is possible for all of humanity.

I have seen hate transformed into love within moments when a man in a state of unmitigated rage suddenly became caring and compassionate. I've seen fear be replaced by inner strength and courage when women and men left abusive relationships they'd been in for years; alcoholics with lifelong habits – stop drinking and completely turn their life around; a teen who lived in hate – forgive her parents and heal her body in the process; a businessman diagnosed with clinical depression became healed and find a passion for living – and each momentous occurrence happened after connecting to the infinitely loving and accelerated power that is our true heritage.

When you have been witness to remarkable events like these, you realize there isn't *anything* that's impossible; and, as these points of reference multiply, they change your belief system. When more people see through the eyes of expansive knowing, we will birth a new paradigm that impacts the way we live each day. Imagine: *a world that works for everyone.* Buckminster Fuller,[3] a brilliant innovative thinker was driven by his intention to make the world work for 100 percent of humanity in the shortest possible time. He felt it could happen through spontaneous cooperation. His vision was in advance of the era when it could become reality. Now is that time, unique to history, when everyday people like you and me can evolve into a society of conscious individuals; empowered to accept the responsibly for designing and shaping our lives.

a world that works for everyone
Once the power of infinite intelligence breaks through the paralyzing patterns of doubt and fear that have crippled our true abilities, we are able to *choose* new directions that embrace our highest aspirations. Becoming aware of unconscious beliefs – frees you – you have *access* to choice. Where before, all that was available was the self-imposed bias passed down from a society that simply hadn't reached a level of consciousness to see beyond the illusion.

Many of you already live and breathe the paradigm *a world that works for everyone;* some of you are not quite there but are open to new impressions and discoveries, while others think it's too big of a leap. I get it. I do. And, I'm not asking you to buy into anything you don't agree with. Just consider what you read in this chapter as food for thought and discussion. Everyone is welcome and invited to the banquet.

our future has not been written
We are in the midst of evolutionary change – for some people *a world that works for everyone* is as inconceivable to imagine

as it would have been for our forefathers in covered wagons to envision a world powered by the technological advances that are commonplace today. It's especially challenging to regard when the crises of humanity are so prevalent: the meltdown of global financial markets and increasing poverty, the natural disasters causing famine and extinction, the continuance of wars and ever-heightening corruption, the oppositional nature of political parties, and the countless countries where no one seems to know how to move toward common solutions. How interesting that this level of turmoil coincides with an ability to access a dimension of consciousness not previously available to the masses...

what we are being offered at this time in history is the most extraordinary possibility ever presented to humankind
Sometimes we are given insight into avenues of unlimited potential that are exciting but seem too BIG to handle. So we just walk away, leaving the responsibility to someone else; a leader who has more power and capability will do what's needed. Right? This kind of thinking is outdated. Today, *we* make it happen. Joining together, while still retaining our individuality, because we each have something to bring to the banquet. *We make it happen.*

The best approach I've found happens when we express ourselves and take action from higher learning, accessing the *profound Energy of consciousness* and applying the *practical and advanced knowledge* we've discovered. Less overwhelm. More simplicity. Connection to the magnetic field of possibility where creation occurs will accelerate the life circumstances we've envisioned. Let's start with an overview: the convergence of logical, practical knowledge with creative experiential wisdom from scientists, world leaders, visionaries, and ancient teachings. Then we'll move into a ground level method of how to begin.

a new way to view what's possible

What would it be like if you lived from your highest potential, surrounded by people accessing an awakened mind and open heart? Ervin Laszlo, Mikhail Gorbachev, Paolo Coelho, and other global leaders have contributed to writing a handbook with answers; filled with concrete solutions to implement radical and positive change in the 21st century. *You Can Change The World* [4] details the universal rights and changes that a new consciousness can bring and the crucial steps needed to bring about this reality.

From the logical to the creative; consider the conscious difference between a caveman and a modern man of today – what would an evolutionary leap of similar significance look like moving forward? Barbara Marx Hubbard, a prolific author and social innovator, quoted by Buckminster Fuller to be '… the best informed human alive regarding futurism…', 44 years ago had an evolutionary vision for our planet that set new standards for social structures – redesigning them to radically advance the quality of our lives:

> … the air cleared, the waters became pristine again. … every basic social system shifted simultaneously as innovations and breakthroughs connected. Systems of health and education, economics and the environment began to coalesce seamlessly by the same powers that orchestrated the creation of the Universe. [5]

idealistic, implausible, or… possible

Why is it that when a person envisions what others can't yet see or don't agree with, their ideas are often dismissed? I'm sure many of you have had this experience, as being on the leading edge of anything is never very comfortable. Cambridge biochemist Rupert Sheldrake would most likely agree, as his work regarding the existence of a new 'morphogenetic field' (M-field)[6] was highly controversial.

Roger Bannister redefined the unthinkable when he broke all records running a four-minute mile, proving again the phenomenon that once we move beyond the inconceivable, it quickly becomes the norm for others as well. In scientific terms this is when a new M-field is born. I believe we are approaching humanity's evolutionary leap through a similar window of opportunity now. David Walonick, PhD[7] reported on a variety of actual studies regarding Sheldrake's findings in this area:

> Harvard psychologist William McDougall (1927)[8] ran a series of experiments beginning in 1920 to study how rats performed in a T-maze. Each generation of rats seemed to be able to learn the maze faster than the previous generation. In fact, after twenty-two generations, rats figured out the maze ten times faster than the first generation had. Even more astonishing, rats who were not offspring of the trained rats, also acquired the enhanced learning ability. In other words, *it appeared that information was somehow being transferred*, although there was no contact between the rats.
>
> Scottish researcher F.A.E. Crew (1930)[9] set out to disprove McDougall's results. Crew's rats picked up where McDougall's had left off. Even though a completely different set of rats was involved, they seemed to have acquired the knowledge of McDougall's rats. Australian researcher W. E. Agar (1938)[10] ran a similar set of experiments for twenty-five years with identical results.

If the M-field theory is correct, then human development may involve more that we usually believe. **If new thoughts and behaviors were to somehow become habitual in a sufficient number of people, it would become increasingly easier for other members of humanity to 'tap into' this information.**

Biologist Lyall Watson (1979),[11] coined the term 'hundredth monkey effect' to describe the critical mass required before information transfer could occur. While studying Japanese monkeys in the 1950s, he observed that when a sufficient number of monkeys learned a new skill, it quickly become part of the repertoire of all monkeys in the colony. Even more remarkable though, the new skill simultaneously became part of the repertoire of other monkeys that lived on different islands.

Each person who integrates the life force Energy of peace to flow through them makes a difference – and joins in the birth of an M-field where that shift in global consciousness can occur. Will we be the ones to activate it? *If new thoughts and behaviors were to somehow become habitual in a sufficient number of people, it would become increasingly easier for other members of humanity to 'tap into' this information.* I believe it is already happening; the question is – will you take part by being one of that 'sufficient number of people' who sparks this marker in the evolution of humankind?

determining your fate

My grandfather was a pioneer who believed what many thought an unattainable feat at the beginning of the 20th century. In 1932 he became the first aviator to cross the Atlantic from Europe to America. He was given a ticker tape parade in New York City in celebration and was invited to meet with President Herbert Hoover at the White House. Yet, when he decided to learn to fly, his family thought it ridiculous, they were so upset no one spoke to him for months. It didn't deter his vision and eventually his family celebrated his accomplishments as though they had welcomed his ideas from the beginning.

We are all pioneers, and as we accept and exercise the power available to us, we will discover that we are the people who can bring peace to this planet – inner and outer. We each have an ability to determine our fate. You can redefine what is possible. And you can do this through all the colors of your personality. Now is the time.

the ground level view – the practical

Inner peace lives out loud as well as in still moments. You can have a glass of wine with dinner and not feel like you're being disingenuous. You don't have to change your entire life, become a vegetarian, give up all your bad habits, and give all your money to charity to participate in this evolutionary movement. By inviting this field of potential into your life you're creating this new world, just by living life more consciously.

You are the perfect expression of you right now: the loving,

funny, caring, sometimes foolish, overwhelmed or anxious you
– inviting the greatness within to emerge. The most enlightened
mystics and sages had unique personalities, so why not you?
You can have a bad day and still elevate humankind by your
vision and stand to make a difference. Once that spark is ignited,
transformation happens layer by layer – with exponential shifts
occurring along the way.

What does living at your highest potential, progressively
advancing higher consciousness look like? You are powerful
and thoughtful, compassionate *and* assertive, courageous *and*
peaceful. You listen to other points of view while looking for
synergistic solutions that magnify harmony for attaining peace.
You initiate cooperation that inspires and stimulates innovation
beyond what you have ever dreamed.

what you can do now

Be committed *and* take action. Be playful and share what's
possible in the best way you know how. Your vision can be as big
as your imagination and it can be as simple as a sincere prayer
for more love and peace to enter the world. I love imagining a
world without war, where the prevailing peace is thought of as
the norm. I love imagining new systems in place where nature
and all living things can coexist and flourish. I love imagining
every person communicating from an awakened mind and open
heart, a world community that recognizes the inherent value
in each person. What do *you enjoy imagining*? What is your
vision? What can you intend that makes you smile just to think
of it?

Consider the possibility that this M-field generating the
world you want to live in, can only open when you become a
part of it. Only you can be responsible for setting the stage of

a transition that includes your design. Here are a few steps to assist in the process:

The Practice for Creating Inner & Outer Peace

IMAGINE PEACE: Commit mentally and emotionally to your vision of **A World That Works for Everyone**.

SHARE LOVE & Live in Awareness daily by asking yourself three questions:

- Are my thoughts loving and peaceful or innovative and inspiring?
- Does this action encourage synergy, creativity, and solutions?
- Are the words I'm speaking empowering, caring, and kind?

STAY CONNECTED to the power of peace in you. **Add Stillness and The Three Breath Awareness** as a daily practice to expand your vibration of consciousness.

If you can answer 'Yes' to these questions – you are designing your life to have meaning, purpose, and fun. If you can say 'Yes' on a daily basis – you are creating *a world that works for everyone* just by *being* you. You are opening that M-field that can ignite the most extraordinary future possible for you and everyone in our global community. Imagine the possibilities...

It's that simple and that profound.

Imagine Peace

Share Love

Stay Connected

Just by committing to being in awareness of your thoughts and actions and reconnecting daily, allowing Stillness to guide you will have an astounding effect on the collective consciousness. Together we can initiate a wave of cooperation that inspires and stimulates innovation, embraces the Love at the core of every person, and entrains a new era of peace.

Thank you for your courage, commitment, and beautiful heart. What an amazing ride we are on as this extraordinary future comes into reality.

With Great Love,

ACKNOWLEDGEMENTS

Where to begin... so many teachers, so much gratitude, so much love circling through the student/teacher and teacher/student relationships that we have in our lives. I understand now how incredibly instrumental both my mother and father were in laying the foundation for my life's path. When I was 13, my mother presented her most important wishes to her three kids, "I want you to find God in your life. I don't care how, or what religion you choose – and I suggest you try them all. I just hope you find God."

Maybe that's why my life's education was such a cultural mix of religions and spiritual paths. Her instruction served me well, and I thank you, Mother, from the bottom of my heart for not placing a box around where love exists.

My father taught me the power of belief; that you can do whatever you *believe* is possible, which he did, studying to become an attorney at 40 while supporting a family of five. Instead of understanding that his addiction to alcohol had robbed our relationship, I hated him for years thinking he was the cause of my leaving home at 16. I know you did the best you could, Daddy, thank you for being a catalyst in my life's journey.

The pain this caused me severely affected my health, causing me to seek out masters of healing. Thank you, Mary Burmeister and Pat Meador, for offering love, not judging a hyped-up cocaine user, and for teaching me through Jin Shin

Jyutsu how energy flows in the body could bring astounding healing that would also open my mind and heart. And, thank you, Howard for demonstrating how energies of illumination can arrive in the most uncommon of packages.

Extraordinary masters of meditation who live by truths of love and compassion might not be easy to find in one's life. I found two. Thank you, Baba, for my initial awakening into the greatest of all journeys – and for the immense love given. Thank you, Gurumayi, for always inviting me to step into a bigger picture; and though I often resisted, your love for me, and my love for you continually guided me forward. Thank you to all the great sages of every religion and spiritual path who sent guidance in my darkest hours.

My dear Panache Desai, I am grateful for our entwined destiny and the love we shared, assuring our steadfastness on the path while magnifying that field of transcendence. May the love you are continue to ignite even more in this world.

My blessings go out to the many experts and traditions whose words and books informed my world; scientists whose discoveries of consciousness educated me of their holistic relationship to spiritual teachings, the many healing disciplines demonstrating the mind-body connection, the new thought teachers whose tapes lived in my traveling seminar vehicle – Esther Hicks whose authentic voice was so fun it made learning to get unstuck easier, Stephen Covey, Landmark Forum, Tony Robbins, Warren Bennis, Wayne Dyer – thank you all for fostering an education that supported me in developing a methodology that has transformed so many people's lives.

To my dear friends whose love gave me the encouragement I needed at each turn in the road: Aviva Fields, angel of mercy, Patricia Lanza, adventurer in life's global travels, Minda Burr,

Lorraine Dellarosa, Rika Hoffman, and Kerry Anne Aldridge, I am forever grateful for your loving support, and to Pedram Hasid for being my knight in shining armor. Thank you to my former partners: Shawn Taddey for demonstrating that one's overall life is more important than any momentary career, James Egan for forcing me to face my insecurities through your unabashed love.

Thank you to my editors, publisher, agent and support systems; Joanna Pyle, Duncan Baird, Susan Mears, Pavel Mikloski, Michelle Zitt, Merryl Lentz and Damien Senn, whose consistent efforts and enthusiasm sustained me.

To my son, Travis, who has been one of my greatest teachers of unconditional love. Thank you for being a caring companion to such a young mom and to your Oma in her final days. To my former husband Michael, I give my heartfelt gratitude; your love nurtured me, your faith ignited beliefs that I could do whatever I was given, and your generous nature taught me to always put my love for people first. I am forever grateful.

Thank you to all the courageous souls whose stories appear here; your love will inspire many I'm sure, just as it did me. And, to the light of Truth, for allowing me to carry your wonder-filled gifts to this world, I am ever grateful, always and forever in your service. May everyone everywhere be touched by your illumined Love.

ENDNOTES

Preface

1. SYDA Foundation, *Welcome to the Siddha Yoga Path*, 'The Siddha Yoga path was founded by Swami Muktananda, affectionately known as Baba.' http://www.siddhayoga.org/.
2. SYDA Foundation, *Welcome to the Siddha Yoga Path*, 'Siddha Yoga practice and study is guided by meditation master and teacher Gurumayi Chidvilasananda. http://www.siddhayoga.org/.
3. Jin Shin Institute, *History of the Teachers*, 'Mary Burmeister... became a master of Jin Shin Jyutsu. She wrote the first English language texts on Jin Shin and held classes in many countries. With her family, Mary founded Jin Shin Jyutsu, Inc.' http://www. jinshininstitute.com/jin_shin_jyutsu/history.html.
4. See Lynn McTaggart, *The Field* (New York: Harper Collins, 2002).
5. See Jill Bolte Taylor, PhD, *My Stroke of Insight* (New York: The Penguin Group, 2006).

Introduction

1. See Ervin Laszlo, *Science and the Reenchantment of the Cosmos*, (Rochester, Vermont: Inner Traditions, 2006, www.InnerTraditions. com), '... this field is not outside of nature: it is the heart of nature. It is the originating ground of all things in the universe, and also their ultimate destination, p.26.
2. *Ibid,* 'In ages past, the connectedness and wholeness of the world was known to medicine men, priests, shamans, seers and sages, and to all people who had the courage to look beyond their nose and stay open to what they saw. ... Now in the first decade of the 21st century, innovative scientists at the frontiers of science are rediscovering the integral nature of reality, p2.
3. Paramahansa Yogananda wrote about the many extraordinary insights the 'unifying light' offered him in the first edition of his renowned book, *Autobiography of a Yogi* (New York: The Philosophical Library, Inc., 1946), ch14, pp 143–9.

4. See Wayne W Dyer, *There's a Spiritual Solution to Every Problem* (New York: HarperCollins, 2001), p 46.

5. *Ibid,* p56

6. See Valerie V Hunt, *Infinite Mind: Science of the Human Vibrations of Consciousness* (Malibu Publishing, 1996), p93.

7. See Wade Davis, *The Wayfinders: Why Ancient Wisdom Matters in the Modern World* (Toronto, Ontario, Canada: House of Anasi Press, 2009), p7.

The Convergence of Knowledge & Experience

1. See manual by LifeScript Learning founder Ron Willingham, *The Way to Wealth: Rescripting Your Personal and Financial Future* (Ron Willingham, 2008).

2. See Daniel H Pink, *A Whole New Mind: Why Right-Brainers Will Rule the Future,* (Riverhead Trade, 2006), p1.

1: SETTING YOUR HEART/MIND VISION

1. See Stephen R Covey, *The 7 Habits of Highly Effective People* (New York: First Fireside Edition, Simon & Schuster, Inc., 1990), Habit #2, p95.

2. See Anyen Rinpoche, *Dying with Confidence* (Wisdom Publications, 2010) which explores death from a Tibetan perspective of mindfulness.

3. This was a favorite saying of meditation master Baba Muktananda when people attended his Programs.

3: LAYING THE FOUNDATION
Learning, Living, and Loving: The Evolution of The Simplicity of Stillness Method

1. See Stephen R Covey, *The 7 Habits of Highly Effective People* (New York: First Fireside Edition, Simon & Schuster, Inc., 1990).

2. NLP University, Robert B Dilts (developer, author, trainer, and consultant in the field of Neuro-Linguistic Programming, since its creation in 1975 by John Grinder and Richard Bandler), *What Is NLP?* 'NLP stands for Neuro-Linguistic Programming,

a name that encompasses the three most influential components involved in producing human experience: *neurology, language and programming*.' http://www.nlpu.com/NewDesign/NLPU_WhatIsNLP.html.

3. Author & Lecturer Warren Bennis, *About Warren Bennis*, "Warren Bennis is an American scholar, organizational consultant and author who is widely regarded as the pioneer of the contemporary field of leadership." http://www.warrenbennis.com.

4. Anthony Robbins, *Entrepreneur, Author & Peak Performance Strategist – World Authority on Leadership Psychology*, 'For the past three decades, Anthony Robbins has served as an advisor to leaders around the world. A recognized authority on the psychology of leadership, negotiations, organizational turnaround, and peak performance, he has been honored consistently for his strategic intellect and humanitarian endeavors.' http://www.tonyrobbins.com/biography.php, and Anthony Robbins, *PowerTalk®! Personal Results Library*, 'PowerTalk®! is an audio magazine program featuring Tony interviewing outstanding achievers and impressive innovators... such as... Dr Steven Covey; Dr Robert Cialdini; Dr Wayne Dyer; Dr Deepak Chopra; Coach John Wooden, Jay Abraham, and many others.' http://www.tonyrobbins.com/products/personal-achievement/power-talk.php.

5. Abraham-Hicks Publications, *The Law of Attraction*, 'Esther Hicks is an inspirational speaker who dialogs with a group of spiritual teachers who call themselves Abraham.' http://www.abraham-hicks.com/lawofattractionsource/TheLawOfAttractionForeword.php.

6. The Chopra Center, *Deepak Chopra, MD, FACP – Co-founder of the Chopra Center for Wellbeing*, 'As a global leader and pioneer in the field of mind-body medicine, Deepak Chopra is transforming the way the world views physical, mental, emotional, spiritual, and social wellness.' http://www.chopra.com/aboutdeepak.

7. See Michael J Formica, MS, MA EdM in Enlightened Living, 'The Science, Psychology and Metaphysics of Prayer: What Do We Pray For, and Why Do We Pray?' (*Psychology Today*, July 28, 2010).

8. Mayo Clinic, Medical Staff (medical editing team of experts in content development and production, product management, and user experience and design), Meditation: A Simple, Fast Way to Reduce Stress. http://www.mayoclinic.com/health/meditation/HQ01070

9. See Cary Barbor, 'The Science of Meditation' (*Psychology Today*, May 1, 2001).

A Few Basic Principles

1. See Wayne W Dyer, *There's a Spiritual Solution to Every Problem* (New York: HarperCollins, 2001), pp46–7.

2. See David R Hawkins, MD, PhD, *Power vs. Force: The Hidden Determinants of Human Behavior*, (United States: Hay House, Inc., 1995, 1998, 2002), p132.

3. See Mitchell L.Gaynor, MD, *The Healing Power of Sound: Recovery from Life-Threatening Illness Using Sound, Voice, and Music* (Boston, Massachusetts: Shambhala Publications, Inc., 1999), p110.

4. See Lynn McTaggart, *The Field* (New York: Harper Collins, 2002), p96.

The Purpose of This Book

1. Annonline™, *Johanson Biography,* 'Dr Donald C Johanson is one of the world's leading and America's best known paleoanthropologists. Working in Africa, he has dedicated the last 25 years to exploring, discovering and studying the most significant fossil finds ever made in the search for our origins.' http://www.annonline.com/interviews/961204/biography.

2. See David R Hawkins, MD, PhD, *Power vs. Force: The Hidden Determinants of Human Behavior* (United States: Hay House, Inc. 1995, 1998, 2002).

4: THE JOURNEY
Chapter 2 ~ Releasing Resistance or Going Back to Sleep
Way Cool... Selena's New Life

1. See Bruce H Lipton, PhD and Steve Bhaerman, *Spontaneous Evolution: Our Positive Future and a Way to Get There From Here*

from the introduction, 'A Universal Love Story' (Hay House, Inc., 2009).

The Angry Man

1. Tom Stone, expert in the application of biophysics and changing patterns of energy in the human body, *The Past, Present and Future of Coaching,* GreatLifeTechnologies, describes this scientific test conducted by Dr. Deepak Chopra. http://www.greatlifetechnologies. com/PastPresentandFutureofCoaching.shtml.

Chapter 3 ~ Reclaiming Your Innate Power...Connecting with Your Inner Teacher

The Dropped Call

1. *Making a Request* references a Simplicity of Stillness Practice you can find in Chapter 4 of this book.

Practice – Listening to the Messages

1. Oxford Dictionaries, 'Genius, pronounciation: /j_ny_s/. Origin: late Middle English: from Latin, 'attendant spirit present from one's birth, innate ability or inclination,' from the root of *gignere* 'beget'. The original sense 'tutelary spirit attendant on a person' gave rise to a sense 'a person's characteristic disposition' (late 16th century), which led to a sense 'a person's natural ability', and finally 'exceptional natural ability' (mid-17th century.).' http:// oxforddictionaries.com/definition/genius?region=us.

Chapter 4 ~ Creating Your Life with Purpose and Love

1. See Taoist Master Alfred Huang, *The Complete I Ching: The Definitive Translation – 10th Anniversary Edition,* 'Ten Contributions of This Translation,' (Rochester, Vermont: Inner Traditions International, 2010), p.xxv, www.InnerTraditions.com.

Chapter 6 ~ Trials & Tribulations...& Other Bumps on the Road

The Greatest Knowledge

1. See Ervin Laszlo, *Science and the Reenchantment of the Cosmos,* (Rochester, Vermont: Inner Traditions, 2006), p54 www. InnerTraditions.com.

Chapter 7 ~ The Darkest Night
1. Mahavidya, *Posting by Hillary Rodrigues on 11th February 2010*.
http://www.mahavidya.ca/the-epics/the-mahabharata/draupadi/.

Chapter 8 ~ Returning With New Knowledge
1. See Ervin Laszlo, *Science and the Akashic Field: An Integral Theory of Everything* (Inner Traditions, 2007) www.InnerTraditions.com.

Drowning in Dark Seas
1. See Andrew Weil, MD, *Spontaneous Healing: How to Discover and Embrace Your Body's Natural Ability to Maintain and Heal Itself* (United States: A Ballantine Book Published by The Random House Publishing Group, 1995).

2. See Deepak Chopra, MD, *Quantum Healing: Exploring the Frontiers of Mind/Body Medicine* (Bantam Books, 1989).

Practice – Powerful Thinking & Speaking
1. See Deepak Chopra, MD, *Synchro Destiny* (Harmony Books, Random House, 2003), 'Human beings are conscious energy fields, along with the rest of the universe. If you want to change the world around you, you need only change the quality of your own vibration; as you change that, the quality of what is around you changes.' p282.

2. See William A Tiller, PhD *Science and Human Transformation*, Chapter 1: Resetting Our Physics Perspective (Pavior Publishing, 1997), p1 www.tiller.org <http://www.tiller.org>.

3. See Gregg Braden, *The Spontaneous Healing of Belief*, Chapter 2: Programming the Universe: The Science of Belief (Hay House, 2008), pp. 84-85. www.greggbraden.com.

Chapter 9 ~ Serving & Empowering Others
Mystical, Mythological, Modern Goddesses
1. See Lee Sannella, *The Kundalini Experience: Psychosis or Transcendence* (Integral Pub, Revised Edition, June 1987), 'In the course of its upward motion, the kundalini is held to encounter all kinds of impurities that are burned off by its dynamic activity.' p168.

5: WHERE DO WE GO FROM HERE

1. Smithsonian, *Roger Bannister – First to Run a Mile in Under Four Minutes*: 'Roger Bannister's impact on America – and the world – was immediate. The young Englishman changed the perception of human limitations when he broke a seemingly insurmountable barrier: the sub-four-minute mile.' http://americanhistory.si.edu/sports/exhibit/firsts/bannister/index.cfm

2. Bio, *Anne Sullivan Biography – Synopsis*, 'Anne Sullivan was a gifted teacher best known for her work with Helen Keller, a deaf, blind, and mute child she taught to communicate. At only 21 years of age, Sullivan showed great maturity and ingenuity in teaching Keller and worked hard with her pupil, bringing both women much acclaim.' http://www.biography.com/people/anne-sullivan-9498826.

3. The Buckminster Fuller Challenge, *Inspired by Buckminster Fuller.* http://challenge.bfi.org.

4. See Ervin Laszlo, *You Can Change the World: The Global Citizens Handbook for Living on Planet Earth* (Select Books, 2010).

5. Foundation for Conscious Evolution, from the film *Visions of a Universal Humanity* (by Quantum Productions in association with The Foundation for Conscious Evolution, 2010). http://www.EVOLVE.org.

6. David S Walonick, PhD, *An Overview of Human Development Issues*, StatPac Survey Research Library. http://www.statpac.org/walonick/human-development.htm

7. *Ibid.*

8. *Ibid.*

9. *Ibid.*

10. *Ibid.*

11. *Ibid.*

ARTISTIC CREDITS

1. *Intention* Image by heartmath.org.
2. *Experience* Image Copyright Valentina R., 2012. Used under license from Shutterstock.com.
3. *Knowledge* Image Copyright Silver-John, 2012. Used under license from Shutterstock.com.
4. *Healing* Image Copyright Richard Laschon, 2012. Used under license from Shutterstock.com.
5. *Integration* Image Copyright STILLFX, 2012. Used under license from Shutterstock.com.
6. *Empowerment* Image Copyright Realinemedia, 2012. Used under license from Shutterstock.com.
7. *EnLightened Living* Image Copyright Robert Adrian Hillman, 2012. Used under license from Shutterstock.com.
8. *Energy in Body* Image Copyright DeoSum, 2012. Used under license from Shutterstock.com.
9. *Where Do We Go From Here* Image Copyright Dgbomb, 2012. Used under license from Shutterstock.com.

The Power of Peace in You Stillness Session CD
Music Coordinator Marlise Karlin
Lyrics Written and Spoken by Marlise Karlin
Recording Engineer Elizabeth Quintinella and Monte Perrault
Artists & Song Titles
• A Quiet Storm by J. Butler licensed by AmbientMusicGarden.com
• Chakra Five; Blue by Ian Mellish licensed by AmbientMusicGarden.com
• Beauty by Bjorn Lynne licensed by Shockwave-sound.com

Graphic Design & Production   Roger Walton

THE WINGS TO FLY

*Once you have flown, you will walk the Earth
with your eyes turned skywards, for there you have been
and there you long to return.*
~ Leonardo DaVinci

If we give each other the wings to fly
Imagine how high we can go
Never forget what a difference your love makes

it takes enormous courage
and one-pointed focus to stay on this path
the only way out is to go deeper within
what you will discover will astound you

there is a quickening of time
not just that it is moving faster
it is aligning more of the creative power we have
to bring the uncommon into our lives

as you allow infinite Energy to inspire your life
all that you value flows to you
you have to wonder what else is possible

how about anything

don't let a moment pass you by
right here and now
you can know
the power of peace in you

HOW TO CONNECT

Connect at www.ThePowerOfPeaceInYou.com and:

- View pictures and videos of the people in this book
- Get FREE Moments of Stillness to tap you into the peace at your core
- Print out home study guides of the core SOS elements
- Receive FREE gift to support your continued journey
- Download audio and video clips
- View Marlise's schedule of events
- Join the Peace Portal Community
- Connect with Marlise on her Blog
- Visit the store for SOS books, courses, CDs and DVDs

Imagine Peace

Share Love

Stay Connected

Connect with marlise at www.marlisekarlin.com
info@marlisekarlin.com